FREE MEN
IN AN
AGE OF SERVITUDE

FREE MEN
IN AN
AGE OF
SERVITUDE

Three Generations
of a
Black Family

LEE H. WARNER

THE UNIVERSITY PRESS OF KENTUCKY

Copyright © 1992 by The University Press of Kentucky

Scholarly publisher for the Commonwealth,
serving Bellarmine College, Berea College, Centre
College of Kentucky, Eastern Kentucky University,
The Filson Club, Georgetown College, Kentucky
Historical Society, Kentucky State University,
Morehead State University, Murray State University,
Northern Kentucky University, Transylvania University,
University of Kentucky, University of Louisville,
and Western Kentucky University.

Editorial and Sales Offices: Lexington, Kentucky 40508-4008

Library of Congress Cataloging-in-Publication Data

Warner, Lee H.
    Free men in an age of servitude : three generations of a Black
family / Lee H. Warner.
        p.   cm.
    Includes bibliographical references and index.
    ISBN 0-8131-1799-2 (acid-free, recycled)
    1. Afro-American families—Florida—History. 2. Proctor family.
3. Afro-American men—Florida—Biography. 4. Florida—Race
relations. 5. Florida—Biography. I. Title.
    E185.93.F5W37   1992
    975.9'00496073—dc20   92-14238

This book is printed on recycled acid-free paper meeting
the requirements of the American National Standard
for Permanence of Paper for Printed Library Materials.
♾

Contents

Acknowledgments vii

Introduction 1

1. Antonio the Soldier 15
2. George the Entrepreneur 26
3. Work and Family 38
4. Reversal 50
5. George's Defeat 61
6. California 71
7. George's Family 85
8. John the Politician 97
9. The End of Reconstruction 115
10. Afterword 135

Notes 140

Bibliography 157

Index 166

Acknowledgments

This work has had the benefit of counsel and criticism from a handful of willing colleagues. Chief among them is Dorothy Dodd, former Florida state librarian and state archivist. She communicated to me a sense of the value and meaning of what is termed "local history" and made her own vast and illuminating research file available to me. Harold and Carolyn Moser provided the kind of very valuable (and detailed) reading that only accomplished historians and gifted editors can provide. Clifton Paisley and C. Peter Ripley read the manuscript at an early stage and gave advice that aided substantially. Richard Sewell taught me the discipline and the context that made the work meaningful—and possible. Gail Warner provided the understanding—and patience.

The Historic Tallahassee Preservation Board and the American Philosophical Society provided financial support for research, which I gratefully acknowledge.

Introduction
An Essay on the Inarticulate

The Proctor men—grandfather, son, and grandson—were part of a large and vital Southern family. Little is known about most of the family, as little is known about individuals in most black families of that time and place. The three generations of Proctor men, moreover, did not leave any personal material. But their accomplishments were so large that Southern memory—in its own ways—chronicled their achievements and their lives.

The chronicle of memory was Southern romanticism at its best—or worst. Uncritical black descendants and white patricians raised the accomplishments of the three to the level of enshrinement in a local pantheon. Blacks participated to provide proof positive that their ancestors had demonstrated, even in times of servitude, that persons of their color and status were of heroic stature and worthy of emulation. Whites contributed to the legend because it confirmed their belief that they were persons of beneficence who, when they discovered worthy black people, patronized them and held them up as models for those of the race that they believed were less ambitious and less deserving.

But the Proctor men were real, and there was a full dimension to their lives that illuminated the highly negative and cruel status of black persons in the history of the South. Discovery of the full dimension of their lives also provided context for their achievements and tended, in fact, to heighten their meaning. Not the least of these achievements was the heritage of accomplishment that passed from grandfather Antonio to son George to grandson John.

This work seeks to illuminate the lives of persons whose horizons were limited. None, most likely, ever sought more than betterment of their personal and family condition or achievements in a local context. Their heritage, and their condition, prevented the realistic vision of grander achievements. Antonio probably never thought he carried a marshal's baton in his knapsack, George surely never sought to become a captain of industry, and it is doubtful that John lusted after the office of president of the United States.

Despite this limitation of vision, the Proctor men subscribed, in large part, to the Western, middle-class value system, which taught that hard work, personal rectitude, and maintenance of family life would lead to happiness and prosperity. But it did not. Their society ultimately denied them not only a vision of grander accomplishments but the more basic happiness and prosperity that they worked for throughout their lives. That, ultimately, was the tragedy of the Proctor men and of their time.

This work is not biography: essay best describes it. A biography, at least in a traditional sense, is impossible to construct for the three Proctor men. Antonio was illiterate, and from him and his son George only the briefest personal record survives. Only Antonio's obituary may be said to come even close to personal thoughts, and from George there is little more. Interrogatories in court cases, notice of his intent to leave Tallahassee in 1849, and a letter in the *San Francisco Elevator* define that body of material. From John there is more, especially in those documents, often consciously created by others, that recorded his words and reminiscences.

But no personal papers remain from any of the three Proctors: they were, in the context of history, inarticulate. This deficiency prevents biography, for, except in rare instances, we have no record of their thoughts. A record of their actions survives, however, and their behavior can be analyzed. A mere chronology of actions would not satisfy, and it would be quite brief considering the small amount of information that survives for a story that spans two centuries and three generations.

I have supplied the analysis and the rationale for the Proctors' actions, for in my reading of the Proctor record and in my grappling with the context of their lives, a rationale appeared. I have tried, in all cases, to identify and accept responsibility for my suppositions about Proctor thoughts. I believe this rationale illuminates their lives and provides context for our own.

The Proctors were not ordinary mortals. Their attainments, outside the context of race, marked them as different. Antonio was a military hero; George was an entrepreneur and a forty-niner; John was a state legislator and federal office holder. These accomplishments would have left tracks across the terrain of any society. But because the Proctor men were black in a white racist society, their tracks become remarkable.

One cannot generalize from the Proctor experience to the experience of American black society, for the Proctors did not share the status of most others of their color. They did share, to be sure, many of the experiences and attributes of blacks in the United States, but, compared to the accomplishments and status of most black persons in that society, they had climbed to the very top rank, and their successes—and their failures—were their own.

The emergence of the three Proctor men as they appear in this work took a long period of time. I have sought to document that emergence and, indeed, the chapters that follow are both a conclusion and an exposition of process. The sources for the Proctor story are not traditional ones. For all three generations, we must rely mostly on local government documents. Americans, as befitted the centrality of the land-hunger that drove their expanding society, were disposed to keep careful records about it. The instrument was the ubiquitous deed book, a required legal record kept in every county courthouse in the United States. The deed books, with their unique indexes, provide a record for every property transaction that was recorded. To be sure, occasionally someone had good reasons for not recording a transaction but not often, for without an official record there was no sure legal recourse in case of non-performance.

The individual citations in deed books provided very basic information. The seller and buyer were identified, marital status was noted, and the property boundaries were described in detail. If the price was not set forth explicitly, the tax was, and from it the price is easily derived. Finally, the date of the transaction and the recording date were set forth. Beyond that, information was not standardized. The property was often described by use, and improvements were noted. Special conditions of the sale, including payment over time were specified if relevant. If slaves were included in the sale, they were generally enumerated by given name, sex, and age. Reference to previous owners of property was commonplace in the recording process. And the deeds included in the books were not limited to real property; any species of personal property could also be included. Finally, mortgages were often recorded in deed books, even though there was a separate file for them.

Great care was taken to protect the books, for they, and the other legal documents kept by the clerk of the court, were the local society's record of itself. Fireproof vaults (often neither) were constructed in courthouses to house the material. In case of fire they were the first thing saved (or, occasionally, destroyed, if that was the reason for the fire). In case of civil disturbance they might be removed to a safer locale.

As society matured, the records changed. Other files were created: lien files, records of claims and brands, and, finally, the deed books came to be called the counties' "official records." In counties where the chain of land records is largely intact, they often provide the historian's first point of contact for a citizen and his government. Because Antonio and George Proctor accepted their society's reliance on landholding as a measure of attainment and as a way to wealth, each occupied many pages in the deed books.

Other categories of local government records are only slightly less important than the deed books. The judicial records reflected much of George Proctor's activities. Every land-owner appears in the deed books, but only those who have been in court—civil or criminal—appear in the court records during their lifetime. (They may appear in probate records after their death.) These records encompass a variety of forms, the most familiar of which include judgment books and dockets; chancery, civil, and law files; and accompanying indexes.

In George Proctor's case the civil court files provide a very full record of information about his business. As a defendant he had to provide answers to questions about the quantity and quality of his work as well as about his financial status. When he appeared in court as a plaintiff, his cases contain information about the nature of his clients. The pleadings themselves show he secured superior representation, giving indication about his position in society and the regard in which he was held by important white citizens.

Tax records add another dimension to courthouse research. In much of the nineteenth century the assessor taxed and, to some degree, enumerated real and personal property. As a result, if the records are available over a period of time they give some indication of an individual's relative prosperity and growth. Often times, unfortunately, tax records have been particularly ill preserved.

Marriage and death records are another component of courthouse documents. For black persons they are generally not relevant until after the Civil War since slave marriages were not recorded in public documents. Because of the large number of marriages performed during Reconstruction, the documents from that time are often very full, though not always well indexed. County commission and county court records, not critical to the Proctor context, are the final large body of material available to researchers. These, usually in the form of minutes, provide insight into the problems encountered by county government and the method of their solution—or lack of solution.

Taken together, the records and documents form the basis for much of what we know of the Proctor story. Fortunately the Proctors concentrated their lives in three locales: Antonio

lived in St. Augustine and Tallahassee; George journeyed from
St. Augustine, to Tallahassee, to California; and John stayed
in Tallahassee. The Leon County (Tallahassee) records, now
largely transferred to microfilm (which, although it insures
preservation makes the records more difficult to use and often
less accessible), are unusually full and well catalogued. Indeed, with the exception of the first volume of the Leon County
Commission Minute Book and some years' tax rolls, they are
complete. The St. John's County (St. Augustine) records are of
the same category of completeness and importance. That they
provide a record of the transition from an English-Spanish
government to a United States government gives them unique
appeal. The Tuolumne County records (Sonora), at the time I
had access to them, were less well arranged. I believe that
there may well be more information about George Proctor in
that collection, but much of the collection was simply not
available for use.

The use of local government records provides unique frustrations to a researcher. The kinds of documents that exist vary
according to local usage and the requirements of individual
states, and no uniform cataloguing system exists. Cataloguing
is not a requirement at all courthouses, and arrangement and
retrieval—even preservation and retention—may be dependent upon the determination of individual staff. Just as serious, the records are truly local; there is no national catalog or
access.

Seeking information about Antonio and George Proctor
outside Florida was like searching for a needle in a haystack.
In the end, the only reasonable method was to make blanket
inquiries from local and state historical societies. Inquiries to
California led to most rewarding collaboration with James
Abajian, retired from the California Historical Society, and
Carlo Di Fararri, retired county clerk of Tuolumne County.
Both these gentlemen graciously made their research avail-
able to me and in large measure are responsible for my telling
of the California story.

The importance of local government records can be over-
played. They are of minimal use unless the subject owned

real property. But for persons, or populations, who meet that threshold (including inarticulate persons and populations), they provide valuable insights. For the Proctors, courthouse documents provided a base for all else.

Theoretically, state government documents should have been very helpful. Florida's government documents, however, were not simply because of the deplorable state of their preservation. Florida had no state archives until almost mid-twentieth century, and the state library did not adequately fulfill that function. The Florida secretary of state was generally charged with the preservation of archival material, and the kindest appraisal is that all failed. There were, to be sure, mitigating circumstances. Government was small—and familiar—and officials experienced no collecting urge nor perceived a necessity for preservation. The climate, with its excessive heat and humidity, endangered what little was saved.

The documents that were preserved are now well arranged and well cared for. There are, however, very few of them. The Florida legislative files are generally unimportant remnants, suggesting that they were simply irrelevant materials that no one paid attention to. Only scattered references to John Proctor survive there despite his ten-year legislative service. Only one document bears his signature. As a result, his legislative record must be retrieved from newspaper accounts and legislative journals; these, although they carry no record of debates, are vital to understanding Proctor's participation and position on issues.

United States government documents were much more helpful than I had anticipated. In addition to the manuscript census returns, which provide the most basic individual and family data, I consulted four critically important collections. The records of the Committee on Indian Affairs contained Antonio Proctor's petition; these documents gave great insight into George's affairs and plans in the mid-1840s. The records of the sub assistant commissioner of the Bureau of Refugees, Freedmen and Abandoned Lands in Tallahassee, commonly referred to simply as the Freedmen's Bureau, provided very valuable contextual material about Reconstruction in Leon

County. The "Department of Treasury, Collectors of Customs" collection in the National Archives contained the letter book with all correspondence concerning John Proctor's tenure as deputy collector at St. Marks. Finally, although the collection from Freedmans Savings and Trust Company's Tallahassee Office did not contain information about accounts in that office, it did include signature cards: two from John Proctor and one from his sister Charlotte. These documents are much more than signature related and contain crucial additional information. In John Proctor's case the cards recorded information concerning his life during Reconstruction and, incidentally, provided critical evidence of family matters.

Manuscript collections of Florida and those of national political figures had only marginal significance in my research. U.S. Senator Simon Conover, the most likely person to have corresponded with or about John Proctor, left no papers. In the case of Antonio, none of his patrons (DuVals or Westcotts) left manuscripts. The manuscripts of Richard Keith Call (a highly significant friend of the Proctors), to which I was kindly granted access by their owner, Mary Call Collins, do not refer to any Proctors. The John Sherman papers in the National Archives, while not referring to John Proctor specifically, provide much contextual material about politics in the state. Such is the case of the inarticulate.

One of those inarticulate individuals, John Proctor's colleague, John Wallace, did leave a memoir. Much of Wallace's career is chronicled herein in the chapters on Reconstruction. Following the expulsion of black persons from public life, Wallace set about composing a reminiscence he called *Carpetbag Rule in Florida: The Inside Workings of the Reconstruction of Civil Government in Florida after the Civil War*. Most students of the period have contended that he had the help of Governor William Bloxham in composing the work; an unnamed John Proctor interviewer supplied the name of Judge Hilton, Bloxham's brother-in-law, as the helper. Wallace was utterly straightforward about the purpose of his work. It was "intended to prove" that while Florida blacks had been deceived and betrayed by the "carpet baggers" into the "hands of their former masters . . . the ascendancy of the Democratic party to the state government in 1877, has proved a blessing in disguise to the colored people of Florida." That put some distance between him and Proctor. Proctor had more (though not unlimited) faith in the carpetbaggers and less in the Democrats. John Wallace is the sole source for much of the political history of Reconstruction in Florida and, even when weighed against his admitted purpose for writing, extremely valuable. At the beginning of his association with John Proctor, Wallace was clearly senior, and they worked closely together. Wallace was more ambitious, more inclined to put personal advancement over principle—witness his flirtation with the Greenbackers and Independentism—so the two men always differed in purpose. By the end of Reconstruction, Proctor had established his own ascendancy within the party and, indeed, within the local black society. It is, moreover, important to remember that Wallace himself was a carpetbagger: in *Carpetbag Rule*, written after the failure of Reconstruction, he does John Proctor no favors.

Florida's newspapers remain a difficult challenge. The state was underpopulated and the climate, officially termed "humid subtropical," claimed many issues that might otherwise have survived. No collecting agencies worthy of the name were established until well into the current century, and only two relatively complete runs of nineteenth century Florida newspapers survive. The *Weekly Floridian* (under various titles) held sway in Tallahassee from 1828 until 1893. Conservative, Democratic, and often arrogant, it was the official organ of Florida government for most of that time. Because its biases were obvious—indeed well known—it is very helpful and the basis of much serious research into Florida history. It was not only a newspaper for the state; coverage of local events—political included—was detailed. This coverage provided much information on John Proctor in the 1870s.

Some isolated runs of the *Tallahassee Sentinel* have survived; it was edited by white carpetbag Republicans who opposed the Wallace-Proctor wing of the party. The papers that would become the Florida Times Union in Jacksonville appeared during Reconstruction and continue in their combined form to the present day. During much of the period of John Proctor's career the paper was Republican, but its Jacksonville location meant that it did not cover Leon County outside of the capitol. Partial runs of other Florida newspapers are listed in the bibliography.

Use of the newspapers for this work was challenging. No newspapers in north Florida were owned or edited by black persons. And by the mid-1880s, white editors devoted very little space to the doings of black politicians. But before then, from 1868 when it became obvious that blacks were going to be a factor in political reconstruction, significant reportage and editorial opinion focused on blacks. All coverage, obviously, was done through the filter of white opinion, whether native born or carpetbag.

The vital source for this work, especially for George Proctor's life, was oral tradition. John Proctor was the initial transmitter of the heritage. Although he was nine when his grandfather died, John could not have remembered his father; he was only four when George left. But he knew the whole story. Two pieces of reliable written evidence make that clear. The Freedman's Bank signature card and the Langhorne interview confirm that he knew the vital details of his father's life after he left Florida and before he died (without returning) in California.

For the Tallahassee portion of his father's life, John had many sources—his grandfather, his mother, and Henry Rutgers among them. Henry Rutgers died while John was a teenager; that left his mother. His mother was probably not the best source. After George went to California, something happened to their relationship. It may have been as simple as distance, but Nancy did remarry, suggesting an active termination on her part. Sketchy evidence suggests John initially sided with his mother. In 1866, when asked about his parentage, he did not mention his father; in 1870 he simply said his father was dead. It was not until 1882 (when he gave information to J.V. Drake, who compiled *The Florida Legislature (Twelfth Session): An Unofficial Directory of State Government,* that he seems to have begun to explain his father's life; perhaps it was only then that he began to understand. Revealingly, in all John's accounts of his heritage that have survived, he never mentions his mother's remarriage or his father's life in California. He was, obviously, uncomfortable with that part of his life. But John Proctor told the Proctor story for the rest of his life, and it began to be recorded. First notice came in the form of a paper delivered at the recently established Tallahassee Historical Society in 1933. Henry E. Palmer, calling his effort "The Proctors—a True Story of Ante-Bellum Days and Since," brought the piece to the attention of white society. Palmer managed to get the outline of the story correct, but without the leaven of serious research or much sensitivity. His greatest puzzle was how, if George had cared for his family, he could have left them to go to California to hunt gold. The question was troubling since, he asserted, the debt hanging over the family came from borrowing to pay for the trip to California. John knew that that was not true. On balance, the brief paper was more a eulogy to the Proctors who had remained in Tallahassee than an appreciation of the trying circumstances of the "Ante-Bellum" Proctors. Palmer recounted John's career but as a dry record rather than as a magnificent accomplishment. As such, it represented a white patrician attitude, more paternal than racist. Palmer referred to Nancy Proctor as "a good-looking slave girl," giving some clue as to his mind-set.

Senator Proctor told his story three times in 1938. The first time, most probably, was to De Witt Lamb between 16 February and 23 February. Lamb liked Proctor and began his account by identifying him as the "only surviving member of the tumultuous 1885 session of the State Senate." He praised John's "alert mind and unfailing memory." During his talk with Lamb, John claimed that his father had died in California during the Civil War, which he knew to be untrue, and added many details about his childhood. He made it plain that he thought Henry Rutgers was a "good man." The report was fair; Lamb noted that John's legislative record was less than "brilliant" but clearly creditable.

A second interview that year, to an unnamed journalist,

led to a gossipy, informative piece that produced some un-
answered questions. ("John Proctor." In Black Archives. Florida A & M University. Typescript.). The typescript identified
Antonio *and* George as from the Bahamas, introduced Lydia
Stout, and described the lure of the gold fields. It also claimed
that George went to California with Washington Bartlett, accused George of marrying a "half-breed Mexican and drifting
off into Mexico," and established the good nature of Henry
Rutgers. The unnamed journalist described John's legislative
service as characterized by "innate nobility," because he remained "at all times, friendly to the white people of the south."
John, the writer concluded, was a "before-the-war type of
negro, at his best. Few like him remain today."

   That thread was picked up by an unnamed participant in
the Federal Writers' Project who, under the guise of serious
history, also interviewed John Proctor. Although this writer
added some material to the Proctor story, his personal judgments perverted his writing. "In true Negroid fashion," he
concluded, John Proctor had viewed the Civil War and Reconstruction "with little interest and only a sketchy idea of the
part he played in the nation's dream." As for George, he had
gone to California only "for the call of easy money." The writer,
who did note that John was ninety-four years old, was most
impressed by John's serenity: "Negroes," he pronounced, "have
solved the problem of worry by complete indifference."

   Professor J.L. Langhorne, of Florida A & M College,
searched out John Proctor sometime between 1935 and 1940
for his own interview. After his retirement he deposited the
recorded discs in the college's Black Archives where they lay
untranscribed until mid-1991. Although minor parts are not
intelligible, the recording reveals John Proctor firsthand. In
his nineties at the time of the interview, he is mentally acute
and interested in, again, telling the story of his grandfather
and father—and the circumstances of his current life. He is
handicapped only by the limitations of the interviewer. Neither Professor Langhorne or John Proctor showed any interest
in John's public career, John's life after the legislature, his
mother, or his thoughts about his aspirations and frustrations.

Even so, the interview is the most personal insight into the Proctor story. John's vocabulary reveals him to be an educated, experienced, articulate human being. The recordings provide firsthand confirmation of his successes and suggest that he was a forceful person of accomplishment rather than a victim at the mercy of other persons or events.

The oral tradition did not receive full treatment until 1943. In that year Rosalind Collins, née Parker, presented another paper to the Tallahassee Historical Society, which was later printed as "The Proctors—Antonio, George, and John." Parker, a student at the Florida State College for Women in Tallahassee, was, like her predecessors, able to interview John Proctor, who would die in December 1944. But she also had an advantage that her predecessors had not. She received guidance and assistance from a mature, trained scholar: Dr. Dorothy Dodd. Dodd, who had earned her degree under William Dodd (no relation) at the University of Chicago, was state librarian and archivist, which gave her the tremendous advantages of training and familiarity with local sources.

The essay that resulted represented the culmination of the oral tradition, but it also provided the first objective historical research into the subject. It presented the essential facts well and made clear the pathos of the whole situation. It dealt primarily with George, establishing him as an intelligent frontier businessman—handicapped by his color—who ultimately failed. John's career was only broadly outlined. The essay was well-researched, well-written, although very brief, and was widely drawn from for more general articles and books that have appeared since that time.

A final piece of the story came in 1975 when the Tallahassee Junior League as its Bicentennial project undertook to interview survivors of earlier times. John's daughter, Lettie Proctor Hill, was one of the survivors they visited and recorded. The transcript reveals an aged woman of limited vision and a highly motivated, well meaning interviewer handicapped by her heritage and her ignorance of the Proctors. It has marginal value.

Without the oral testimony—almost exclusively John's—

this book would be much leaner—if, indeed, it could have been written at all. It would have been based almost exclusively on the legal records described above. But that is the hallmark of inarticulate populations: they have not the means or the desire to provide the traditional kinds of records familiar to the more literate parts of our society. Lack of recorded information makes their history less accessible, less personal, and, as a result, less well known.

Other documents, as yet unknown, may be discovered that will add detail to the Proctor story, though the nature of this kind of subject is that its sources are not always susceptible to rational search. Fortunately, John, a highly intelligent, articulate human being—a survivor of over a century of American history—carried the story to us. Without that transmission, we would all be poorer.

ONE

Antonio the Soldier

Of the three Proctor men, Antonio, the patriarch, did best. Perhaps his ambition was more circumscribed, although he taught his son and grandson to aspire beyond themselves. Or perhaps it was the time in which he lived; his son's and grandson's maturity came when race was more limiting. Fortune, too, played a part: the patriarch seemed to be in places of opportunity at times of promise. Whatever the reasons, of the three of them, only Antonio did not see his attainments dashed by others.

For the first third of his life he was Antonio Propinos. Born a slave in Santo Domingo about 1743, he may have moved around the West Indies as a young man. At some point he became the property of a British army officer, perhaps in Jamaica.[1] Beyond this, little is known of his early life. But the West Indies were important European colonies in the midst of a mercantile world, and it is important to remember that he came to life in no backwater. And given his intelligence and energy—so obvious from later actions—the logical assumption is that in his early years Antonio was able to rise above the level of other black slaves in that place.

The assumption is borne out by his claim to have been at the Battle of Quebec, 13 September 1759, as body servant to a British officer with whom he had left Jamaica. He probably remained attached to British officers in one way or another, for he next appeared with a different officer in Massachusetts at the outbreak of the American War for Independence. He asserted that he had been in the colony at the time of the Boston Tea Party and claimed to have been present at the Battle of Lexington.

After that event, record of Antonio disappears for some time. He was not literate, he was not white, and he was a slave.[2] Those factors combined to relegate him to obscurity. The best guess is that he returned to the West Indies during or following the War for Independence.[3] He was probably part of the British loyalist community that returned there after the war. This much is known: Toney (as he became known in frontier Florida) in time became the property of Panton, Leslie and Company and was in that capacity (most likely as an interpreter and agent in dealing with the Indians) at some time prior to receiving his freedom in St. Augustine.

William Panton was also of this British loyalist community, albeit at a much higher level. Forced to leave Georgia because of his sympathies, during the closing years of the war he migrated to Nassau where he awaited the outcome. When the British lost, it must have been obvious to Panton that his career in the fledgling United States was not promising. Accordingly, he cast his designs on a new and probably much more familiar location—St. Augustine.

Early in 1776, Panton had joined forces with Thomas Forbes under the name of Panton, Forbes and Company. With offices in Savannah and New Orleans, much of their effort was directed toward the Indian trade in British Florida. In this they were eventually joined by William Alexander and John Leslie, and the name of the company was changed to the more familiar Panton, Leslie and Company.[4]

The company's rapid success, however, was soon threatened by diplomatic trading. In 1784 St. Augustine and the rest of Florida were transferred to the Spanish. Despite the apparent difficulty of the situation, the firm retained its position in the Spanish colony. Indeed, it soon managed to convince the Spanish that it was indispensable to maintaining peaceful relations with the Indians. Accordingly the Spanish government decreed the firm remain in Florida (headquartered in St.

Augustine and Pensacola) and granted it a monopoly on the Indian trade. As a consequence (there was no other mercantile house of significance) it prospered and became, in effect, the banker of Spain's dominion in Florida. Thus, the tie to Panton, Leslie and Company insured that Antonio Propinos was close to the center of events despite his status as a slave.

St. Augustine, then the capital of east Florida, was nothing more than an isolated colonial outpost. It consisted of something less than three hundred houses, about one-half of them constructed of wood. The town itself spread over three main streets along the river, and it was in deteriorating physical condition. The Spanish who came to St. Augustine in 1784 were destined to be no more than placeholders. The English administrators they replaced had introduced many innovations from traditional Spanish methods in government and administration, land management, Indian relations, and economic activity. The returning Spanish never had sufficient power and personnel—and they probably lacked the will as well—to change things. So, as one historian has concluded, "the second Spanish occupation (1784-1821) was only nominally Spanish." [5] If the English changes were not a sufficient problem in themselves, the Spanish administrators also had to deal with the land-hunger of the United States on the one hand and the dissolution of the Spanish colonial empire on the other.

In the eyes of Antonio Propinos, however, the world of Spanish St. Augustine must have seemed remarkably attractive. Given the nature of shifting empires, changing governors, and rotating civil servants, the place must have given an overwhelming impression of impermanence. It was precisely the kind of situation in which an intelligent black slave might expect to do well, perhaps even to leave his bonds behind. (It is worth noting that it was this kind of situation that so benefited Antonio's son and his grandson in middle Florida and that his son consciously sought out in California.)

Antonio's rise to freedom confirms the environment's promise of opportunity.[6] During his "long residence" in St. Augustine, he "experienced many reverses." The clear inference is that there were conspicuous successes as well as failures, and it is clear that it was during this period that he changed his name to Proctor, gained his freedom, married, and raised a family. He and Serapia Edinborough were wed in 1798. Children came apace, the eldest in 1799, and the youngest in 1819. (The names of three are known: Josepha, George, and Antonio.) The father became a land owner, a slave owner, and a person of some celebrity.[7] As his obituary would put it, "his conduct was such as to command the esteem and respect of . . . the inhabitants, as well under the administration of the United States as the dominion of Spain."[8]

There is no explicit record of how or when Toney Proctor gained his freedom. Some sources declared he purchased it; others state that it was given him as a reward for outstanding service. Certainly his freedom (and his family's), whatever its motivation, came prior to 1816; it may have come as a result of his actions in the Patriots' War (an attempt of Georgia frontiersmen in 1812 to acquire Spanish territory), an act for which he was later granted land. Precise knowledge of Antonio's act is lacking. Most likely it was Antonio who carried to neighboring Indians a vital message that was responsible for staving off Spanish defeat.

In 1812, in a filibustering action, American citizens had laid siege to St. Augustine; it was obvious that left to its own defenses, the city could not break the siege. In these critical circumstances, a "negro" from St. Augustine who spoke the Indian language managed to travel to the Indian villages and convince them to aid the Spanish against the wishes of the Americans. The "fine" talk of the Americans, the Negro told the Indians, "was to deceive and amuse you, they are going to take your country behind the St. Johns [river], the old people will be put to sweep the yards of the white people, the young men to work for them, and the young females to spin and weave for them." Then, in the words of one of the chiefs, "after the Indians heard the talk of the Negro they believed it."[9] This "incitement" and the actions that followed, in the mind of one careful student of the conflict, "tipped the balance in favor of war and against the Americans. It set in motion a chain of events that lifted the siege of St. Augustine and ended the immediate threat to the Spanish colony." [10]

It is not, of course, absolutely clear that the intrepid black was Antonio Proctor; the man in question was not named. What is clear is that the Spanish government rewarded Proctor for a meritorious act described, officially, as "so well known" that "no one was unaware of it." Proctor, the citation continued, knew the Indian language "to perfection," and his action had to do with the "neighboring Indians" with whom he had "influence." Finally, according to the citation, Proctor was not a member of the militia, leading one to believe his services were more of an individual nature. In conclusion, the citation pointed out that Proctor's services contributed to the "pacification of this territory." For his act, Antonio received 185 acres of land. [11]

Because of the absence of any other claimants, it seems evident that it was Antonio who secured the Indian aid. Certainly the event was consistent with his later reputation. He continued, moreover, to work with whites and Indians for the next two decades and was of considerable service to the Americans during the Seminole wars as an interpreter, scout, and guide.

If Antonio were indeed the messenger to the Indians, that action would have made him a person of distinction in St. Augustine. The importance of such notoriety, however, lies in the effect of Antonio's fame and status upon George. Born in 1806, George was just coming to the age of awareness and understanding at the time his father received his rewards. Because the date of Antonio's manumission is not known, it is unclear whether or not George was born free—at the very least he was free by the time he was ten years old. Since the document providing Antonio's reward identified him as free, it is evident that manumission came earlier. George was most likely born free, or his free status came so early in childhood that the event was unknown to him.

Lacking any direct testimony, there is no way to definitively describe the relationship between father and son. This much is known: in 1819 George and Josepha Proctor were identified as godparents to Antonio and Serapia's youngest child,[12] suggesting a strong family relationship in 1819. Also, George remained closely associated with his father until at least 1849, indicating that the connection between the two was intimate and lasting. Finally, there is no indication that when Antonio and George moved to Tallahassee in the mid-1820s any other members of the family accompanied them. The conclusion is clear: father and son were bonded. Antonio's attitudes, thoughts, and ambitions likely became George's. Antonio's example became the underpinning of George's life. In great part that consisted of the attitudes, thoughts, ambitions (and hoped-for accomplishments) of Western middle-class society.

Antonio must have been an ideal father to George, loving, interested, and successful. He was also black. He was described in Spanish documents as a "moreno libre," a free moreno. In usage common to St. Augustine at that time, moreno meant a pure Negro or at least very dark skinned.[13] There was no light skin to make Antonio, or George, rely on light color to expiate their heritage. Antonio gave George, in other words, a contradictory and ultimately damning gift: the intellect of a Western middle-class white person and a skin color that made that ideal impossible. It might have worked in Spanish colonial society, but it would not in nineteenth-century United States.

The Spanish were, the testimony is complete, committed to an elaborate system of racial consciousness.[14] The bonds of black slavery were explicit and firm. Yet, as David Brion Davis explains, "for all their racial consciousness," they were "distinctive in their final acceptance of the inevitability of intermixture." In practical terms that meant that whites and blacks alike viewed the system as not being a closed one—unlike their American neighbors to the north.[15] The suggestion is that the Proctors' opportunities were not so limited in St. Augustine as they might have been in an American environment. Race was a disability, but it was not wholly damning. There was flexibility in regard to color, and it was precisely that limited flexibility that made Antonio's new position possible.

According to George's testimony, he was born 12 May 1806 in St. Augustine, one of Antonio and Serapia's middle children.[16] Except for George and Antonio, little information survives on any other members of the family after 1816, and the information on these two for the next fifteen years is scant. It is unclear if Antonio ever worked the land he won in 1816. Certainly he was not known for his agricultural pursuits. He did, furthermore, purchase his house in St. Augustine, suggesting that he did not work the land.[17]

For the Proctors the next significant event was the change of flags. It had been obvious for some time that Spain would lose and that the United States would gain Florida. Now the timing had been settled. For the Proctors the change in sovereignty was fraught with uncertainty. American attitudes concerning race and the operation of its system of slavery were well-known; it was much more rigid and oppressive than the Spanish system. Proctor, moreover, had won his standing with Spanish authorities. The trick would be to make the transition without losing status—a difficult thing at best. Making the situation more difficult was the American attitude that Florida blacks were especially dangerous because of the relative freedom they had enjoyed within the lax Spanish system. The Americans seemed determined to impose their own system of racial control completely and quickly.[18]

There were some moderating conditions. The treaty between the United States and Spain was to some degree ambiguous about free blacks. The most logical reading makes it seem as if their "privileges, rights and immunities" were to be maintained.[19] While this was not a guarantee, it seems to have set the tone for free blacks already in Florida who remained in the territory. Obviously it had nothing to do with blacks who came to Florida after the change of flags. Also, Antonio's status and reputation under the Spanish undoubtedly helped. The population in St. Augustine did not change overnight; some Americans were there before the shift of sovereignty, and some Spanish remained after. These people knew Antonio, and they obviously did not rethink their opinion or treatment of him. Finally, of course, there were Antonio's obvious abilities. He spoke the three languages requisite for the area, he was traveled, and he was experienced. He had been one of the instruments by which the Spanish dealt with the Indians, and it was to the Americans' great advantage to use him in the same role. In that sense he represented a vital element of continuity. This must have been crucial to the Americans who were now responsible for dealing with the Indians.

Antonio Proctor made the transition to the new order well. By 1820 he had purchased his house on St. Francis Street, one block from what had been the Spanish barracks. Built in the 1770s and often used as rental property, it was a three-room house with a two-room detached kitchen. It was in poor repair and not in a good area, although the lot was fairly large (66 feet by 144 feet).[20] Still, the purchase was significant: it made Antonio a landowner in the city and established his household there, certainly a position of status for the former slave.

By 1823 Antonio had come onto the payroll of the Territory of Florida in his own name. Between sometime in 1822 until at least 1 December 1824, he was hired at irregular intervals as an interpreter, messenger, and aide in dealing with the Indians. It was during this time that he worked closely with Governor William P. DuVal who was notably impressed with his character and ability.[21] There also appears to have been a later period of service as an interpreter in the early 1830s.

DuVal was a former congressman from Kentucky who had been appointed a judge by President Monroe. He prospered in Florida. He was a man of some learning who had the affection and respect of literati such as Washington Irving and who was dynamic and determined enough to enjoy a leadership position in the rough and tumble life of the new territory. President Monroe appointed him governor of the territory in 1822.

It was during this period, as well, that Antonio became identified with Dr. William H. Simmons. Simmons was a physician from Charleston who had moved to St. Augustine in 1821. He was a man of substance, highly thought of throughout the new territory. Indeed, he was one of the two commissioners chosen to select the site of the new capital (which would be, of course, Tallahassee). Although Simmons owned land across the street from Proctor's house, there is no record of how they came to know each other or as to the precise nature of their relationship.[22] There are, in fact, but two documents connecting the two.

The earliest is from 1824 when Antonio sold his 185 acres: Simmons witnessed the sale. Then, 1 October 1826, Simmons appears in documents as guardian of Antonio's son, George.[23] Both documents, especially the guardianship, show a close relationship between the elder Proctor and Simmons. Furthermore, they not only confirm Antonio's position within the new American society, they also offer evidence of one of the ways in which he maintained his position. (His son George would successfully emulate that means later in his own career.)

By acquiring as his patrons, and undoubtedly his friends, men like Simmons and Governor DuVal, Proctor went far toward buttressing what might otherwise have been a tenuous position. In an age of white supremacy, he sought protection and refuge from whites of power and substance. He could not have chosen better.

Notice of Simmons's guardianship came when George was apprenticed to Daniel McQuaig in 1826 to learn carpentry, a practice not uncommon in the South at that time. In standard manner, the contract specified that at the conclusion of the apprenticeship, George was to receive a bench and tools. (For unexplained reasons, the document identifies George as having been born in 1810. This may have been done in an effort to make him appear to be four years younger than he actually was.)

The apprenticeship lasted but two and one half years of the agreed-upon five and at some point carried George to Tallahassee. It ended abruptly: early in 1829 the Leon County Court, in an action called the *Territory of Florida* v. *Daniel McQuaig* or *Ex Parte George Proctor, a minor,* v. *Daniel McQuaig,* ended the contract. By way of an affidavit Toney (who probably was still in St. Augustine) complained to the court that McQuaig was about to leave the territory, contrary to his understanding of the apprenticeship document. The court answered by giving

George over to the possession of Governor DuVal for the remainder of the contract term. All these events made clear the Proctors' place in their society. On the one hand there was the status indicator of apprenticeship: a young black man was bound to a white in the Deep South. And, were there any question, a prominent citizen of St. Augustine and the governor of the territory were standing by. Most of this came, obviously, from Antonio's position rather than George's, but the result was clear. George would have a trade to follow, and father and son had friends in high places, heady stature for Floridians of their color.

It appears that Antonio too left St. Augustine by 1830. (At this point all mention of any other members of the family ceases.) Antonio's name begins to turn up as a property holder in Leon County by that time, and he disposed of his last property in and around St. Augustine in 1830. George was in Tallahassee by the beginning of 1829, more or less permanently.[24]

Seen in retrospect, the move was probably more than aimless. Although the precise motivation is not clear, one important factor must have been the realization that St. Augustine was no longer at the center of things. Antonio and George seem to have been particularly aware that their best chance for success was at the center of the social and political circle rather than on the perimeter. Governor DuVal and the government had gone to Tallahassee. St. Augustine was and would continue to be an anachronistic backwater in the new American scheme of things. Life was obviously precarious for blacks in such a place, especially if powerful friends had moved away. In Tallahassee, by way of contrast, Antonio and George were protected and, by the mid-1830s, prosperous.

George Proctor was permanently handicapped by the fact of his heritage, mental and physical. That alone was responsible for the tragedy that befell him. Yet the tragedy was also defined by his early success. It is hard to imagine a more hopeful beginning for a black person in the Deep South than the one that George Proctor enjoyed. Born of Antonio, a respected free black of great reputation, he was apprenticed in a

Antonio the Soldier 25

legitimate trade as the ward of the governor of Florida. No other black in the territory had those advantages. Nor did the advantages and successes end there: they would continue and build until they made his downfall a tragedy of particular consequence.

TWO

George the Entrepreneur

The Tallahassee in which George began to practice his trade, and where he would spend the first half of his adult life, was a raw frontier community. The site of the town had been selected in 1823 and lots sold to the public in April 1825, immediately after the initial survey was completed. Tallahassee's growth was explosive. One early settler observed in late 1825 that "a year ago, this was but a forest; now there are more than a hundred houses, two hundred inhabitants, and a newspaper."[1] By 1830 the population would reach 926 (541 whites; 381 slaves; 4 free blacks) and a decade later 1,616 (815 whites; 786 slaves; 15 free blacks).[2]

The rapid population growth makes clear the area's attractive reputation. Although Tallahassee did not lay on any transportation route—in fact, it was hard to reach—and, although it was not distinguished by some striking natural land form, it was the territorial capital. It was, moreover, in the midst of north Florida's fertile crescent, which became prime cotton-growing and later slave-holding country.[3] But, fundamentally, at a time when ambitious citizens of the young republic were on the move with their seemingly self-generating society, Tallahassee was another attractive and logical step in the moving line of frontier settlements.

The first wave of Tallahasseeans had distinct, if diverse, origins. Most of those who became leaders were from the Upper South, especially Virginia. William DuVal, the governor who befriended Toney and looked after George, was from the Old Dominion. Thomas Brown led a caravan of family and slaves from his plantation in the northern neck of Virginia; he became the second governor of the state. Francis Eppes, Thomas Jefferson's grandson, came in 1828. There were other Upper South states represented: the Calls and Walkers came from Kentucky; North Carolina produced Chaires, Crooms, and Branchs; Maryland sent Randalls and Wirts. They were conservative, patrician, and usually Episcopalian.[4]

The United States Army provided many early Tallahasseeans. The 1830s witnessed the Florida chapter of Indian removal in the second Seminole war. Although there were no battles or forts in Tallahassee or Leon County, some effects of the strife were evident since Tallahassee was the capital. While stationed in Tallahassee, army personnel were a distinct population. One clerk who had migrated from New England commented that instead of being in the field, army officers might "be found basking in the sunshine of the city." In their native North, he observed, they "were considered as blackguards or anything but respectable members of society." In Tallahassee, however, they had been "suddenly converted into gentlemen of the first water, . . . not by any worthy conduct of their own— but by the unseen power wielded by military buttons and epaulets."[5] The jealousy was evident but so was the impact of the temporary population.

There was also a foreign component that added to the strange mixture. The Marquis de Lafayette owned a whole township of land on the eastern boundary of Tallahassee, a gift from Congress in July 1824. Although he later sold his land to raise cash, his initial approach was to found there a slave-free, utopian community. In March 1831 fifty to sixty Norman peasants took up the venture. It soon failed, but a majority of the newcomers settled in or near Tallahassee.[6]

The largest group of these early Tallahasseans were people without position or property who came to Florida looking for opportunity. Whether referred to as yeoman farmers, ordinary citizens, or whatever, they were the sinew and spirit of the frontier's cutting edge. These had the usual qualities shared by all those who would leave established communities in response to the call of the new. These groups together produced a unique mixture. Of those who migrated to Tallahassee before 1850, forty-seven families represented the Lower South, seventy-two families started from the Upper South, thirty families were from the North, and thirty-two families were foreign born.[7]

One other population component in Tallahassee deserves particular mention: the legislators and government officials. Once a year, usually in the winter, they swelled the small town for the annual legislative session. They provided a special atmosphere and made the town more susceptible to the vagaries of social and political opinion.

As if the varied and shifting population were not enough to imprint Tallahassee with a particularly unsettled aura, so did the early years witness crucial and telling special events. Three in particular deserve note. First, the people of Tallahassee suffered episodes of yellow fever in 1831 and 1841. The 1831 siege was the less serious, but it gave the region a reputation for sickliness. The epidemic of 1841 was far more worrisome: the best estimates suggest that the population was literally decimated. The "visits of the Angel of Death," explained an editor who had recently buried his wife, "had been sudden, tragic and common to all ages, both sexes and every class of society."[8]

The weather was just as capricious. September 1837 brought a tropical storm, and while it seemed serious at the time, it proved to be only a precursor of worse events. In October 1842 a hurricane swept the area, and a year later came the climactic storm with a tidal wave that destroyed Port Leon, Tallahassee's shipping outlet on the Gulf. A decade later came a third storm that brought more heavy damage to the town.[9]

Then there was the fire. In a hastily constructed village where wood was the dominant building material—and where there was no building code or organized fire department—the danger was obvious. The inevitable catastrophe came 25 May 1843. Fire burned the entire business district. "The inscrutable Providence" had, intoned the mayor, inflicted an "awful calamity."[10]

There was one other ingredient in Tallahassee's character: violence. The 1830s appear to have been a particularly lawless period.[11] A pillory stood in the center of town, and a gallows was in use before 1830. Neither appears to have had much effect on the populace. Assaults, duels, and murders were commonplace. One foreign visitor observed that "the habit of carrying arms was universal." It was only after 1841, when Francis Eppes was elected mayor, that the situation changed. A strong and moral leader, he awakened an obviously waiting citizenry to action. New ordinances were passed and enforced. As a result a later observer noted that although a "year ago you could not walk the streets without being armed to the teeth," it was now "different."[12]

In other words, Tallahassee in the 1830s and early 1840s was a society in flux. The town had no tradition or feeling of permanence. The same characterization might be made of St. Augustine during Toney's residence or the Reconstruction Tallahassee of John's era. A rapidly growing population of diverse background in a new area confronted with violence and catastrophe—such was not designed to produce a pacific or structured society. It was obviously not so bad as to repel newcomers, for they continued to arrive and put down roots. The attractiveness of the place still outweighed its negative features.

The Proctors were well-positioned in Tallahassee. Toney had first made his acquaintance with the area by 1824 and was closely identified with Governor DuVal. In the mid-1830s when he was in his eighties, he would be recalled to military service by Governor Richard Call because of his experience and his stature with the Indians. His son George, apprenticeship behind him, was ready to begin his career. A young man of obvious talent and intelligence, he was able to do well in Tallahassee's fluid society. Had the society been one of some age with rigid castes and traditions (as would develop a decade later), it would have been very different. Ira Berlin, who analyzed those mature communities, pointed out that "elite free Negroes . . . at the top of black society . . . did not fully escape white rule." There was a rigid three-caste system.[13] Surely the outlines of that system were present in the 1830s Tallahassee, but they were not yet fixed. Proctor occupied a position between slaves and white men, but in the 1830s his life was characterized by the opportunities rather than the constraints of the middle position.

Tallahassee's fluid nature was nowhere better illustrated than in its land values and attendant speculation—a phenomenon that attracted many people, George Proctor included. The original land sale in 1825 had been at auction, and it may be unfair to use its prices as a good measure of value. But the north addition to the city was quickly platted and opened for sale in April 1828. The land sold quickly, usually at five dollars per parcel and increased rapidly in value. Some plots sold for one hundred dollars within the year, and a decade later (before the depression) commonly sold for at least two hundred dollars without improvements.[14] That kind of increase suggests that optimism was rampant. Opportunity was abundant for anyone, and there was little thought of placing restrictions on people like George so long as there was no overt challenge to the system itself. All his actions fit that requirement.

George grasped the opportunities enthusiastically. Little is known about his work in the early 1830s. The scheduled end of his apprenticeship would not have come until 1831. The best assumption is that he began practicing his trade at about that time. Undoubtedly his first work was piecework, either as a subcontractor or for patrons. Certainly there was demand for that kind of service. At his age, with no substantial independent experience, George could not have begun building houses with a crew in his own name—regardless of who his sponsors and protectors were.

He was obviously very successful in his craftsmanship and in its business side. Two events before 1840 give positive proof of that judgment, and the events also offer insight about George's operations. The most striking was a newspaper advertisement that appeared 6 January 1838: "For sale, Lot No. 101, lying on Calhoun street, adjoining the residence of J.B. Bull, and is a beautiful situation. On the lot is an elegant and commodious new two-story Dwelling House, and all necessary outbuildings. . . . For further particulars, call on the subscriber and proprietor. G. Proctor."[15]

Almost as startling was a Superior Court decision of 13 May 1839.[16] With the highly respected Thomas Baltzell as his attorney, George brought suit on 16 October 1838 against Leah Bryan for five hundred dollars. The cause of the action was clear. On 14 June 1837 Proctor and his business partner William Weeden had rented two horses, a wagon, and a "cariall" to Bryan for ten days at a price of fifty dollars. It seems that Bryan returned the items in poor condition, without full payment, and that one of the horses died shortly thereafter. Proctor collected $251 for his suit. .

Building the house and bringing the suit were themselves remarkable for a free black in the Deep South, especially since Proctor won the suit against a white person. Even more remarkable, however, was what the two actions revealed about Proctor. Most important, by the beginning of 1838 he had established himself as a member of the adult community. The house on lot 101 NA, in an upper-class white neighborhood, was a speculative building. Proctor had purchased the property 13 October 1836 from Ezekiel Freeman, a white man, for $350.[17] When he sold the house and property in March 1838, the price was $3,510.18.[18] The clear conclusion is that in an eighteen-month period, Proctor had not only constructed a rather substantial wooden dwelling but that he had been able to finance it. Given the knowledge of his background and Tallahassee business operations, the best guess is that he borrowed the money. Even assuming the loan had come from a friend or sponsor, the amount involved makes clear the degree of trust in Proctor's character and ability. That degree of trust was, of course, magnified by Proctor's status as a free black.

The case against Leah Bryan points to the same kind of appraisal. The fact of note is that by the middle of 1837 Proctor was in business with a partner, and the partnership owned equipment that it was able to rent out in slow periods. Like so many other young men of his time, George Proctor eagerly embraced the entrepreneurial ideal.[19] It was what his young society taught, and he was an eager learner. Much of the reason that his color was not inhibiting was within him: he was bright, skilled, ambitious, and energetic. The time and place were also important. Opportunity, for all, was abundant; competition was not restrictive but, because of demand, exhilarating. And, of course, he was the son of Antonio and had been a ward of the governor.

There is further confirmation of Proctor's achievement in the 1830s, arising from evidence that was of a potentially restrictive character. In January 1833 one of Leon County's representatives to the Florida Legislative Council presented a "petition of certain persons in Tallahassee praying a law to prohibit free negroes from contracting as master builders." The measure died in committee. The object of the petition had to be George Proctor. Clearly he was making his mark in Tallahassee, and just as clearly there were elements of the population who at this early date foreshadowed the hardened racial attitudes that would dominate in later decades.[20]

Additional information about Proctor's activities in the 1830s is found in the records of his land transactions. Between 1830 and 1840 he purchased nine city lots, most in the expanding northern fringe of the town. Some he may have acquired in the expectation of building on them. Others, it seems apparent, he purchased only to sell as the price rose. In 1833, for example, he was able to buy the property at 237 NA at a tax sale for $1.25; he sold the lot for $65 in early 1839. Other parcels show the same kind of operation.[21] In one case the profit was smaller, and on one property, of course, he built a house. Three remaining lots were bought at the end of the decade and became tied up in his disastrous court battles of the 1840s. But with those three exceptions, Proctor made money on his small-scale land speculation.

George's other projects in the 1830s are much more difficult to identify. In the next decade his tracks would be clearer, not only in the county clerk's land records but also in the court records. One suspects that most of his clients began going to the trouble and expense of recording their contracts with him in order to assure legal recourse if there were problems. If this were indeed the case, part of the change grew from people's harsh experiences during the depression. Another reason for the change was that Proctor's financial status was by then open to question.

Proctor's building projects in the 1830s were almost entirely unrecorded. His son John named him as the builder of three very similar houses on McCarty Street (later East Park Avenue) between Calhoun and Gadsden streets. This was in a developing white, upper-class neighborhood on the eastern edge of town. John explicitly identified the structures as six-room houses, each with an outbuilding, woodshed, cistern, and well.[22]

These projects would have been substantial undertakings for George, especially that early in his career. Still, his house on 101 NA and the legislative petition show that he was capable of that kind of work, and the known record of his projects in the 1830s leaves time for the construction. In 1992 there were four houses on that site; three of them date from the period 1837-1842. Of the three houses in question, one, the Knott house, built of wood, was originally a two-thirds Georgian house with a basement and two floors above ground level, a six-room house. The Murphy house, also wood, had only a basement and a first floor but may well have had three rooms on each floor. The Chittenden house, built of masonry, had a basement and one and a half stories above ground, perhaps six rooms.

Thus all of the houses may have been six-room structures, but they were not of the same configuration, and one hesitates to use the term "similar" in relation to size. Yet all had basements or ground floors, a feature common to other Proctor houses. Also, George built in both wood and masonry, and the size is similar to most of the houses he built. Given the accuracy of John's recollections and these similarities, it is possible that George did build these structures. (Another possibility, less likely, is that there was another structure on the fourth lot that disappeared.)

The most likely explanation, however, turns on an error in John's memory. If the three sisters were in fact built on the south side of McCarty between Gadsden and Meridian— rather than between Calhoun and Gadsden, a difference of one block—then there is corroborating evidence.[23] In April 1838, Henry Bond, a successful local businessman, signed a contract with George that turned on ownership of the property between Gadsden and Meridian. The most logical reading of the contract is that Bond (who owned the property) had contracted with Proctor to build houses on the property and advanced him a thousand dollars for materials and labor. If, at the conclusion of the work, Bond wished to dispose of the property, he would then collect the notes from Proctor and transfer the property to him. In any case it is obvious that there were small houses on the parcels by the beginning of 1839. Bond, by the way, kept the property.

Despite the lack of clarity about the three structures, the case for their construction is strong. The important conclusion is that the three sisters, in combination with the house on 101 NA, establish George Proctor's solid reputation. Fresh from his apprenticeship, he had plunged into his trade and proved his capabilities as a craftsman and a businessman.

Much of Proctor's success was directly related to his construction business. Certainly just as important were his friends, patrons and sponsors. He had the good fortune to have William Simmons as his guardian in St. Augustine and in having his care assigned to Governor DuVal in Tallahassee. Both of them were men of the first rank, socially and politically, in the new society. The reason for that connection may have been Simmons's and DuVal's appreciation of Toney, but they were obviously comfortable with George. For him it meant that as a black in white society, he had powerful support. It is hard to conceive of how he could have done better than to have had the governor as his protector. George was obviously aware of the effect of such sponsors, for throughout his career he showed an uncanny ability to repeat the situation.

His legal position was at best precarious. The frontier society gave him room to maneuver and made his otherwise exposed position tenable. But he was also liable, as he must have realized, to unexpected reversals. In the 1830s and 1840s, continuous attempts to restrict free blacks' activity and freedom were largely successful. Indeed, by 1860 the free black population of the state had shrunk to but 606 or 1.5 percent of the total population. But George was of a special class since he had been a free Spanish inhabitant before the change of flags. It is worth remembering that he did pay a white poll tax and pleaded in court as an equal of white men.[24]

One of the legal restrictions placed on free blacks during this period was that they were required to have a white legal guardian: oral tradition assigns such guardians to George. If this were true, no legal record remains, and, moreover, it may be that Proctor was not required to submit.[25] But he must have realized the practicality, indeed virtual necessity, of maintaining close identification with powerful white men. At least his career in Tallahassee shows that he managed that feat without fail.

The early power structure in Florida centered around a half dozen of Andrew Jackson's cronies. Known in Tallahassee as the Nucleus, they were a particularly conservative bunch. At the center of the group was Richard Keith Call, twice territorial governor, devoted Jackson admirer, and later a fervent Unionist. Call was an able and ethical man and his pro-bank conservatism eventually led him to a painful break with Jackson. He and the Nucleus then quickly became the conservative, pro-bank party in the territory. In Tallahassee they were especially powerful and would remain a force in territorial and state politics.[26]

George's closest identification was with this group. Oral tradition specifies that Call, and later George Walker, his partner, were among Proctor's "legal guardians." Although that is open to question, and although little documentary evidence of a close relationship remains, it is very likely that Call and Walker were among Proctor's friends and protectors.[27] The meager documentary evidence that survives points to cooperation in land speculation in town lots and financial backing in at least one of Proctor's building ventures.[28]

George had significant dealings with other members of the Nucleus, notably Leslie Thompson and Richard C. Allen. Thompson, one-time mayor of Tallahassee and law partner of socially prominent Thomas Hagner, at times opposed Proctor in court. But, significantly, George retained him at least once for his own legal business, and the two made land deals.[29] George's dealings with Richard C. Allen, and subsequently his son Benjamin, were primarily financial. It is very probable that the Allens loaned Proctor money for his building projects, and shortly before he left Tallahassee, Proctor was renting and sharecropping Benjamin Allen's land.[30]

Proctor had other benefactors. They too were politically conservative and appear to have been divided between the forming political parties. From among the proto-Whigs, there appears to have been a project with L.O'B. Branch, nephew of Governor John Branch, for constructing a house. Simon Towle, Whig mayor of Tallahassee and comptroller of the state in the late 1840s and early 1850s, represented Proctor in court. Simmons and DuVal, of course, were of this party, as was Proctor's later prime benefactor, Henry Rutgers.[31]

Given the attitude of this class of men, and given their political preferences, it was no accident that Proctor found most of his friends and benefactors among them. Patrician and patronizing, they undoubtedly found George Proctor more deserving of their time and efforts than did Democrats and men of less stature. But the significance of Proctor's reputation and position lay precisely with the status of these men.

Proctor had friends in the Democratic party as well. Romeo Lewis recorded three business dealings with Proctor. Lewis was sheriff of the county and at the center of the local Democratic party. Later, when Proctor found himself in so much legal trouble, his most-used attorney was James Westcott, Jr. Westcott, bulwark of the Florida Democratic party, served as territorial secretary and temporary acting governor prior to statehood. With the coming of statehood, Westcott became a United States senator. It is worth noting that after Westcott became senator, he does not appear as Proctor's attorney of record, perhaps because he spent so much of his time during the Tallahassee court sessions in Washington.[32]

The exact chronology and extent of these relationships is less important than their existence. So long as he had identification with, and to some degree protection from, these men, George Proctor maintained his freedom of action within Tallahassee. Ira Berlin has pointed out that many free blacks "owed their privileged status directly to connections with white merchants and planters." [33] In George's case other significant factors were involved, but certainly the white connection was important. And he exploited that connection by maintaining several white friends and making sure that they were not limited to one political faction. The 1833 legislative petition to the contrary, he appears to have made no significant enemies. In all places where accounts of ill feeling ought to have appeared, they are absent. But it was more than just absence of malice. Proctor clearly enjoyed a special condition. The matter of the extraordinary status with the white poll tax, and court proceedings confirmed it. He was unique in Tallahassee.

The other factors that aided Proctor's success in the 1830s were just as important. The frontier town's population was most un-Southern, and economic opportunity was abundant. So long as that was true, freedom of action for free blacks was considerable. It was only later when frontier characteristics gave way to majority and when the character of Tallahassee's population shifted and the town became conscious of its Deep South location—and neighbors, that it became a Deep South town itself.[34] Finally, of course, there was Proctor's ability. He was a good carpenter, and he managed his financial affairs competently. In a growing town, this went far to assure success.

For a white man, of course, not all those factors would have been necessary to assure a large measure of success, and the attainments would not have stopped at a given line. There remained, that is, a limit on even George Proctor's attainments. But, for a free black in the Deep South, it was necessary to have all these factors operating in order to succeed. George Proctor did that, and as a result the 1830s were for him a decade of optimism and progress. The next decade would see the changing realities of his condition destroy that optimism and promise.

THREE

Work and Family

Tallahassee in 1840 was still a small village, serving as county seat and territorial capital. The settled area comprised a grid about eight blocks long (north-south) by five blocks wide (east-west) on the top of a gentle ridge two hundred feet above sea level. The masonry capitol, then about half finished, was at the south edge of town, and three blocks north of it stood the three-story masonry county courthouse. The business district that occupied the area in between was largely constructed of wood, which was readily available and cheap, and uniformly one to three stories tall. The residential districts surrounded the government and business establishments.

There were three church buildings by 1840—Methodist, Presbyterian, and Episcopal—although other denominations utilized temporary meeting places. A market house, a school-house, and a Masonic lodge rounded out the town in concert with two hotels—the Planters and Brown's. As Southern frontier towns went, it was typical, having only the brief, annual legislative session to challenge the comparison.

The next decade brought two kinds of physical change. First, the town expanded rapidly. The prestigious residential neighborhoods grew to the north along Calhoun Street and to the east on McCarty Street (later Park Avenue). At the same time there began to be more masonry structures, especially in the business district after the disastrous fire in 1843, but the new structures were about the same size as the old.

The other great change was in the economy. The panic of 1837 hit late in Tallahassee; it was not until mid-1839 that the downturn was evident. It became serious very rapidly. The city, whose finances were always precarious, had to issue scrip to maintain itself.[1] Then the financial ripples began to spread; by 1841 and 1842 notices of bankruptcies crowded the columns of the town's weekly newspapers, and in the spring of 1844 the Union Bank of Florida failed. When these harsh realities were coupled with the fire, sickness, and storms of the early 1840s, it must have seemed to many in Tallahassee that the fair promise of that area had been blighted.[2]

In at least some respects, however, the disasters of the early 1840s were a kind of cathartic: the economic mess produced some reform, and the rebuilding resulted, in one contemporary's evaluation, in a "well-arranged and commodious" fireproof brick business district. As one perceptive recent writer put it, "the fire marked the transition of Tallahassee from a frontier community to a pleasant Southern town."[3]

George Proctor contributed significantly to the expansion of the town: the frontier entrepreneur responded to the growth demand. From the evidence that survives, it seems clear that he was almost constantly at work building in Tallahassee for most of the time from the mid-1830s until spring 1849. The list of his projects that we know of is impressive: the major jobs include two substantial masonry dwellings and eight substantial frame houses.[4] George also had continual smaller projects: a "bake house" for a confectioner, a grist mill and barn, additions to houses, and, in one case at least, a grave marker. Of these structures, only three survive today, one masonry house and two frame houses. Two other frame houses survived until after 1940.

George built primarily in wood. Given the time and location, this was normal. Good wood was abundant and cheap. The land around Tallahassee abounded with virgin yellow pine. It had unusual strength, natural decay and insect repellent qualities, and was easy to work. The normal procedure from the 1840s until the Civil War for building wood structures in Tallahassee was straightforward. The carpenter would purchase milled timbers locally. Then with his crew he would frame—and usually floor—the house. For siding, window assemblies, and all architectural woodwork, he would purchase millwork that had been imported from the North, usually of white pine.[5] Tallahassee and all of north Florida simply did not have mills capable of producing fine woodwork at that time. Occasionally mahogany or some other especially chosen material was used for fine interior work. George fit the mold of Tallahassee's typical carpenter.[6] Evidently, he sometimes used native milled boards for exterior siding, but this appears to have been his only deviation from the pattern.

Masonry construction was less familiar to Tallahasseeans, and for good reason. There was no acceptable local stone, and local clay did not produce good brick. Very little antebellum brickwork survives in the town, and most of what there is has been cement washed or stuccoed. Finally, there was the problem of time and expense: importing northern brick—often required for foundation work—took both. It was little wonder that wood became the dominant construction material.

Nevertheless, whether for reasons of permanence, aesthetics, or prestige, there were some masonry structures. The courthouse and the capitol were brick, though the capitol was cement washed then scored to look like ashlar masonry. And George Proctor built at least two masonry structures. The Chaires mansion at 336 North Monroe Street survived until the mid-twentieth century. George built that two-story house for Lawrence O'B. Branch, nephew of Governor John Branch, in the early 1840s when that location was on the northern edge of the town.[7]

The other Proctor masonry structure is the Randall-Lewis house at 424 N. Calhoun, built either just after or at the same time as the Chaires mansion. The buildings were one block apart. There is not as good a documentary link between Proctor and the Randall-Lewis house as there is with most of his other work, but the circumstantial evidence is very strong, and oral tradition is quite persistent in linking the man and the building. In any case, the Randall-Lewis house was among George's finest works. Built on a slight grade, it consists of a ground floor of four rooms with a central hall and a principle floor of the same number of rooms with an entrance slightly above grade. The top floor is restricted by the roof slope to two rooms. Originally a federal portico decorated the entrance. The design and workmanship are outstanding. The workmanship is easy to account for, but the question of design is more troublesome. Most of Proctor's work was of undistinguished design. It was simply no better or worse than houses other builders constructed at the same time. They were functional, cheap, and attractive. Likewise the Chaires mansion, for all its size and craftsmanship, was not of outstanding design— which is not to say that it was unattractive or that it was a failure. But the Randall-Lewis house—and to a large degree the Rutgers house, which came later—represented a different level of design.

Both of these structures were built for the same man, Henry Rutgers.[8] Rutgers was a New Yorker who had come to Tallahassee in the 1830s. He served for a time as treasurer of the territory and then became cashier of the ill-fated Union Bank. As did other males of his standing, he served his terms on the Tallahassee city council. Later, Rutgers would become the local agent of the Southwest Railroad Bank, and, of course, he engaged in the universal frontier practice of land speculation, although with a moderation that was unusual for Tallahassee. In the late 1840s and throughout the 1850s, Rutgers would be Proctor's special friend and protector.

The logical assumption is that Rutgers in some way aided George in the design of these two structures, both of which may have been residences for him. Both had federal porticoes, and the windows and blinds on the front are identical. They share the same floor plan—although the Rutgers house has only two levels and is constructed of wood rather than masonry. The dimensions of the two houses may have been identical. Their width is still identical; modifications to the Rutgers house make its original depth difficult to establish. Both buildings had an attractiveness and timelessness about them that, ultimately, aided in their survival.[9]

Less is known about most of George's houses. The Chaires

mansion was evidently among his largest projects. Surviving photographs show that it was five bays wide and four bays deep, with a full two stories and a very shallow hip roof. An abundance of architectural woodwork at the roof line and windows, combined with the shallow roof and rectangular front, gave the house an Italianate look. Much of this woodwork, obviously, was not original.

George's other wooden houses that we know of were utilitarian. Most of the houses George built were probably either four- or six-room buildings typical of Tallahassee in that time. One common plan was to include two second-floor or attic rooms on top of the basic four-room first floor. This was probably the arrangement in the "three sisters" construction and was, in fact, duplicated in the Randall-Lewis and Rutgers houses. The house George raised for Isaac Robinson in 1841[10] was 40 feet by 28 feet with a center hall running 28 feet. At the front of the house were two 16 feet by 16 feet rooms, and to the rear the rooms were 12 feet by 12 feet. The agreement with Robinson was to "frame and raise" the house in twelve days for a hundred dollars, with Robinson to furnish the milled lumber.

The common method of construction, and one that George followed in all cases, was full timber framing. Balloon framing had only recently been invented, and the culture lag was especially noticeable in Tallahassee. Balloon framing would not become common in Tallahassee until well after the Civil War. Lap joints, and mortise and tenons were used to join the framing timbers in all cases, the joints held firm with cylindrical wooden pegs, 1 inch to 1½ inches in diameter. Flooring was usually pine, "secret nailed," tongue and grooved boards, commonly 1 inch to 1½ inches thick. Lap siding was usually without fancy millwork and often of cypress, valued for its weathering quality. Roofing was very often of pine shingles. Tin and metal roofs were usually reserved for larger buildings, though occasionally they were used on dwellings. Slate was rare in Tallahassee—so far as is known there was only one slater in the town—but George built at least one house with a slate roof.[11]

It is difficult to estimate how long most projects took from inception to completion. The Robinson house took twelve days to "raise and frame," but that was not typical since it included neither site and foundation work nor any finishing. The house at 101 NA evidently took about one year to complete. Proctor purchased the property in mid-1836 and was advertising the completed structure by the beginning of 1838. Allowing a six-month preparation and planning time, the one-year figure results, but it would be for a total and finished product—and the builder's first such project at that. The masonry houses may have taken longer, but it seems reasonable to say that most of Proctor's houses were probably done in a period of six to eight months.

George Proctor was not a lone carpenter putting up houses. He was a frontier businessman speculating on growth, and his business was construction. Ultimately, of course, he failed as a businessman but succeeded as a craftsman. As a businessman, Proctor in many ways was like his white contemporaries. In the 1830s he and his partner William Weeden, another free black, operated under the name of Proctor and Weeden. By the mid-1830s they had built up a stock of tools and implements for use in their trade and their business.[12] They would either build for other people under the usual working conditions—as with Henry Bond and the "three sisters"—or build speculatively themselves.

It is unclear how long the firm of Proctor and Weeden continued. During the time the firm was in existence, each man seems to have done independent work as well, and in the 1840s Proctor was operating under the name of George Proctor and Company.[13] Weeden evidently left Tallahassee before Proctor did.

The problem of a work force or crew presented Proctor with a unique difficulty and foreshadowed his ultimate failure and the reasons for it. The hard truth was that, free or not, Proctor was not white, and he lived in a racist society. It seems clear that whites did not work for him. There were at least two reasons: no white man could permit himself to be in an inferior position to a black, and it would have been dangerous for Proctor if they had. This would have made it appear as if a black were directly competing with and challenging the very basis of the established Southern social order. Proctor, as his other actions showed, was too intelligent and wise to do that. For the same reason, and others, Proctor could not form his crew exclusively from free blacks. Such action would have raised Proctor and his workmen to an exposed position in white society, and, besides, there were simply not enough free blacks in Tallahassee to do that.[14]

There was but one option left: use of slaves. The question of whether or not Proctor owned slaves lacks a definitive answer. In 1840 his household is shown as consisting of seven free black males and one free black female. (At that time he was married but without children.) The census also shows him with six slaves in the household. By 1844, the next year tax records are extant, he is recorded as being without slaves or free blacks. In 1845 he is taxed for five slaves and no free blacks; in 1847 for five slaves and one free black; and in 1848 for six slaves.[15] (By that time there were his five children and his wife in the household, probably the six in question.)

Whether or not Proctor owned slaves, it is clear that he rented or leased them for his work crews. The evidence is explicit: in 1839 he "hired" the "negro man (named Jack)" from Joseph Albertson, and in 1842 he hired "Pompey" for thirty dollars per month from P. L. Edwards. Likewise, in at least one instance, a white man hired a slave from Proctor: Thomas Brown and John D. Galbraith hired Solomon in 1835 for $235. Finally, Proctor rented "negroes" from Benjamin Allen in 1848.[16]

Use of slaves, whether leased or owned, confirms Proctor's thoughts about himself and his future: business and ambition came before anything else. He was free: his father had left the bonds of slavery behind. Opportunity was abundant, and the proslavery orthodoxy had not yet fixed itself on Tallahassee. For him, as for white slaveholders, slaveholding was not a moral but an economic issue. There is, for example, no record of George Proctor ever manumitting a slave. At least at this period, George thought of himself as entrepreneurial man rather than black man. If he intended to achieve his goal, economic forces dictated that he have a labor force, and societal forces dictated that the labor force be black. There was no alternative. The inherent contradictions in his position were not yet evident, and it is unfair to fault him for not foretelling the future. His motivation was so strong, however, that it would leave him no escape when the confrontation came.

The number of persons in Proctor's crew appears to have usually been four to six. The 1840 census suggests that number as does an interrogatory in an 1841 suit against him. That interrogatory specified that Proctor had four or five "boys" in his crew.[17] (Contemporary usage in Tallahassee suggests that this meant males from early teens to fifty.) In any case, that size crew with the kind of direction that Proctor appears to have been capable of giving, was adequate to produce the kind and number of structures he built.

Proctor's ability was unquestioned, and he solved, temporarily and at unknown mental cost, the problems of a work force and operation in a white society. Other problems defied solution. Money was one. Proctor's family was poor; he did not have his own capital. Societal attitudes were even more important and, ultimately, controlling. At their simplest, these attitudes raised skepticism about free blacks. By the early 1840s, as cotton growing became more profitable, and, as there was an enhanced need for slaves to produce cotton, slavery came to be justified on racial grounds. As black skin came to be a badge of social and moral inferiority, the position of free persons with black skin became tenuous. The great inhibition to this group of persons came not in overt moves but in more insidious, indirect restraints. White society could not admit so damning a contradiction as a successful free black. It moved, despite the loyalty of George Proctor's white patrons and sponsors, to limit his success.

It is hard to conceive of how George could have become a wealthy man—or even a financial success in the 1840s. Perhaps had he been twenty years older he might have accomplished it in the Tallahassee of the 1820s or 1830s when slavery—and race—were less important, but it was impossible for any free black of the 1840s.

George Proctor carried on his business with borrowed money: his heritage, his position in Tallahassee, and his recent successes gave his white patrons reasons to make capital available. In some jobs, obviously, capital was not required. That is, when he worked for an owner who supplied materials on his own property, George was hired only for his services and the labor he provided. But this method of work had smaller financial rewards—and probably smaller psychological satisfaction as well.

The way to prominence—and wealth—was in speculative building, banking on the growth of a frontier society. Proctor followed the path of his white contemporaries in this regard. But like his white contemporaries without capital, he was forced to rely completely on borrowed money to finance his operations. Record of most of Proctor's financial dealings has not survived. Clearly most of his notes of indebtedness were privately held and repaid. There was no need to record these documents. The operation of credit machinery was much less formal on the nineteenth-century frontier than elsewhere, and, in the case of a free black borrowing from patrons, it appears to have been even less rigid.

When Proctor needed large sums of money, he probably turned to one of his friend-patrons—Call, Allen, Rutgers, or Walker. There is only scanty evidence of these transactions,[18] but Proctor continually needed large sums of money, and there was nowhere else to go. These transactions between friends were, of course, precisely the kind of borrowing that would not have been recorded at the courthouse. At other times, however, Proctor went into the open market for smaller sums of money. The court records are full of these notes in the instances where Proctor, or one of his debtors, fell delinquent, and there is every reason to believe that this kind of borrowing was a standard practice.[19]

His method, once he had decided on a specific project, appears to have been quite simple. He would borrow as much money as he needed to combine with his own resources to reach whatever level of participation was required of him. (At times he was not responsible for the total project. His participation could range anywhere from simply providing labor to complete personal direction and financing of a speculative venture.) When the project was concluded and he was paid, he would proceed to settle his debts. In the case of his legally recorded debts, his individual obligations ranged from $2,000 to $135.83. Most of these notes held against him seem to have ranged from one hundred dollars to four hundred dollars, and when larger sums were involved it was often because one creditor had acquired (through endorsement of his notes to others) several of Proctor's notes.[20] But it is important to remember that he usually had several notes outstanding at one time; indeed, when Proctor fell short of cash, determining the priority of these notes was often a particularly vexing problem.

But throughout most of the 1830s, Proctor and most of his contemporaries were blissfully unaware of the hard years ahead for all of them. Proctor had mastered the skills of his trade and managed well the unique problems of being a free black in a white society. He must have been flushed by his early success and impressed with the heady optimism by 1839, or he would never have taken the momentous step he did.

On 8 May 1839 George Proctor married. His bride was Nancy Chandler, a twenty-four-year-old slave owned by Mary Chandler, a twenty-four-year-old widow from Maryland who had moved to Tallahassee.[21] Three weeks after the wedding, in an action obviously agreed upon prior to the marriage, he purchased Nancy from Mary Chandler.[22] Those actions were crucial, for they, and the manner in which they were carried out, went far toward determining George's future.

As with all his business dealings, Proctor did not have enough cash to complete the transaction outright: as was his usual practice, he signed a note. In this case, the price was $1,300. Proctor paid $450 cash and signed a personal note for the remaining $850 to come due within twelve months. The note was endorsed by two young white men of some standing in the community, Alexander F. DuVal and John Demilly. The very existence of the note and the cosigners, of course, testifies to Proctor's reputation in the white power structure. It was also significant that the marriage ceremony took place at St. John's Episcopal church, for this was the church of the socially and politically prominent. It was, in a sense, a kind of imprimatur on the union and the people involved. The marriage, although evidently happy and obviously fruitful, produced problems from the beginning. Most conspicuously, there was never any manumission recorded for Nancy. It is unrealistic to think that George Proctor could have overlooked such an important action. He had paid careful attention to such things throughout his life, and error here was simply unthinkable. What seems much more likely is that so long as Nancy was mortgaged, she was considered property. There was very little law governing that kind of situation, and, in the face of stiffening white attitudes, property rights took precedence over other considerations. With sufficient assets George could have prevented this situation. But he was not liquid so he resorted to his accustomed pattern—borrowing. After all, it had always worked in the past, and his familiarity with use of slaves may have dimmed his sensitivity to the danger—or moral issue—in this case. Proctor did not know that a choice was required. Like the American dream he chased, he thought he could succeed at all he tried. His father had, and he had. Prosperity reigned, and anything and everything was possible.

Yet a choice was required. It was not made, and it was ultimately damning and clearly emblematic of George Proctor's condition. Success was not possible. As an entrepreneur, even though his finances were under control throughout the 1830s he continually suffered cash flow problems. He was never able to accumulate sufficient capital to make the transition from using his manual skill and labor to produce income to using his capital investments and managerial ability to generate income. In George's case, the hard times following the panic of 1837, solely on racial grounds, prevented his success: bankruptcy laws held the still-mortgaged Nancy and the family hostage, and George was unable to pay the ransom.

Despite the debt burden and the uncertainly of Nancy's position, the union appears to have been a happy and good one.

Nancy was pregnant soon after the marriage and gave birth to
Florida within the year. That child soon died, but Charlotte
was born 16 March 1841, Georgianna (or Georgia Ann) on 2
August 1842, and John Elias on 13 January 1844. They were
followed by Mahaimen Steward (later called Bahamia or
Bahama) on 1 June 1845, Mary Magdaline on 13 June 1846, and
George on 13 July 1848.[23] It is clear that the Proctors lived
together in a family relationship that was as close to normal as
their peculiar status permitted. Their separate household was
known as that and accorded a sanctity that accompanies independence. They were frequent enough churchgoers at St.
John's to have their children baptized there, although evidently they were not members.[24]

But obviously their marriage and family relationships
were not what were normal for the great majority of Americans in the 1840s. Their very existence as free blacks belied
normality, as did the debt over Nancy's head. Even the church-
going was special. George and Nancy were not members; Nancy's former mistress, Mary Chandler, and George's patron/
friends were Episcopalian. Toney, still healthy, was a "zealous
Baptist," and in the 1860s Nancy and the children went to the
Methodist church.[25] Even church attendance, thus, was dictated by their special status: the limits of their freedom were
narrowly defined. And, of course, those confines would continue to shrink in the 1840s and 1850s until they disappeared
altogether.

FOUR

Reversal

The early 1840s were a disaster for George Proctor. The events of those years dashed whatever optimistic trend his life had, destroyed his career, and made clear his inferior, almost servile, social status. From that point until his death, despite some periods of stability and brief glimpses of hope, his life was one of sorrow and defeat.

Many Americans, of course, had harsh experiences in those years following the panic of 1837. The events of the sharp economic turnaround of that year were not so disastrous. It was, rather, the second shock of 1839-1840 that proved impossible to surmount. The initial panic of 1837, although serious, was short lived. In the South, the situation was made more pressing by an unusually large cotton crop that came at the same time as the drop in demand caused by the panic. Yet there was a quick upturn. The 1838 cotton crop was very poor, and, because of that and financial maneuvering in the northeast, cotton prices rose slightly. Conditions improved even more because of an influx of overseas capital. Governmental spending increased because of the distribution of the federal surplus of revenue from land sales.

But in 1839, just as conditions had achieved this significant improvement, a bumper cotton crop caused another sharp price decline. In the South, banks responded by suspending specie payments. Nine states, Florida included, defaulted on their bond interest payments to foreign investors. This, in turn, caused an abrupt halt to the flow of money from Europe to the United States, bringing an end to those conditions that had halted the panic of 1837. This time there was no happy ending: the depression lasted until 1843 nationally and through 1844 in Tallahassee.[1]

During those years of misery, conditions in Tallahassee were desperate. Defaults were commonplace and foreshadowed the failure of the Union Bank, the town's only bank, in 1843.[2] It failed not only because of its chronic lack of specie and its questionable management policies but because its loans could not be called in, as debtors had no money for repayment. The bank's failure only exacerbated the situation and worsened the plight of many other individuals. Bankruptcies abounded, and sheriff's sales became commonplace. Yet even forced sales accomplished little since prices for material goods were so depressed. The economic misery was compounded by the storms, sickness, and fires of the early 1840s. George Proctor, like most of his contemporaries, stumbled unaware into the morass that no one expected. The hardships following the panic of 1819 had been forgotten, and most people did not suspect that another depression was possible—Proctor among them. Indeed, he seems to have moved into expanded land speculation and increased building activity just before the economic downturn. All this optimism and increased activity, of course, was based on credit. When the panic hit, he was caught short.

Proctor's difficulties became serious when he was unable to satisfy the mortgage on Nancy. The particulars of the transaction were complicated. The original note for $850 was from Proctor to A.F. DuVal; DuVal endorsed the note to John Demilly, and Demilly endorsed the note to Chandler. The reasons for the endorsement chain were not specified, but Mary Chandler was probably leery of doing business with a free black, and the two whites who were in effect co-signers to the note undoubtedly increased her chances for collection. Unfortunately for all parties, DuVal and Demilly were in serious financial condition and not capable of clearing the note.[3] In any case the note was due 1 June 1840 and was not satisfied on schedule. On 6 November 1840 Mary Chandler went into court to secure payment.[4] Obviously leaving no bridges unguarded, she sued all three men for a total of $1,700, a figure that included the $850 principal, interest, and damages. It seemed a clear-cut situation; the defendants did not contest the debt, only its size. The court responded by scaling down the figure to $1,023 but levied it against all three men. The judge further clarified the situation when he decreed that the money had to be paid by 1 March 1842. Nancy was to be foreclosed at that time if the debt was not settled.

Given the economic situation, it is hard to conceive that Mary Chandler believed she could collect her money simply by going into court. The town was small enough so that an individual's financial condition was evident to everyone: DuVal, Demilly, and Proctor clearly did not have the resources to pay. She waited six months before filing the suit, and the next ten years would reveal remarkable forbearance on her part. What seems probable, given the times and similar action on the part of others, is that the widow Chandler went into court simply to give legal status to the debt. It was as if there were now an imprimatur given that the debt was valid and collectible at some time in the future.

The decree setting the $1,023 debt figure was not announced until 22 December 1841. The fourteen months of the proceeding were undoubtedly difficult for Proctor. So far as is evident, he had only a series of minor construction projects during the period, certainly reflective of the economic situation. More serious, during the spring 1841 session of the court, he was hit with five additional suits that would eventually result in judgments totaling $1,544 against him.[5] Although the $1,544 figure was smaller than the sum of the initial total of the suits, the effect on Proctor had to be pronounced. He would, during the same period, recover some $398 through suits of his own, but this figure represented only a minor percent of his obligations.[6] Besides, Proctor was aware that he had at least another two thousand dollars in debts he would have to meet in the following eighteen months.[7]

A crushing blow followed: Mary Chandler went back into

court 13 February 1841, even before the settlement of her suits against Demilly, DuVal, and Proctor for payment of the mortgage, to ask that the mortgage on Nancy be foreclosed.[8] In view of her later actions in postponing a forced sale, Chandler's actions are puzzling. Perhaps she feared that with the five additional suits against Proctor at the same time—and undoubtedly rumors of more to follow—unless she foreclosed the mortgage, Nancy would be sold for someone else's benefit. In that case the move can be seen as something less than heartless.

There is no way, short of Proctor's own testimony, to measure his mental response to the decree. Lacking his written testimony, the best existing measure of his attitude comes from Mary Chandler's testimony in court, this time on 24 January 1842.[9] She claimed then that she had evidence that George was preparing to take Nancy out of the territory, obviously in an attempt to get beyond the reach of Florida law.

Gifted with hindsight, it is clear that flight was probably the best answer to George Proctor's burden. Unlike almost every other free person, he was denied a means to relieve his own predicament, for to declare bankruptcy would be to lose Nancy and the children. The decree of 29 January 1841 foreclosing Mary Chandler's mortgage was indisputable evidence that the law considered Nancy to be George's property before it considered her his wife. Thus had he declared bankruptcy, she and the children would have been considered assets and sold. This was made even clearer when on 24 January 1842 there came a further decree from the court forbidding that Nancy leave the territory.[10]

Proctor was a prisoner of his society and his time—as well of his location. More bluntly, these factors doomed him. Whereas his contemporaries—including his debtors—could wipe out their obligations and start over, Proctor had to pay all his debts at face value, regardless of the fact that his debtors might not be forced to pay him at full value. His wife and family were held hostage by the court. It was injustice at its worst, but it was a white society speaking to a black man and his black slave wife. Nothing could change his color, heritage, and future in the eyes of the law. From this point to the Dred Scott decision a decade and a half later was but a short distance. These circumstances did represent something of a change, but it was a familiar change. The Tallahassee of the early 1830s was fluid and building. Attitudes toward race and slavery—in the South as well as in Tallahassee—had not yet hardened into their prewar inflexibility. But the decade after 1831 changed all that. Cotton became highly profitable, increasing the need for—and price of—slaves. As a result proslavery and anti–free black arguments hardened and matured, and north Florida became committed to the South and its ideals. Tallahassee society, moreover, had matured and lost its fluidity. Finally, the early 1840s were a time of threat and hardship, and the society reacted by retreating into safe defensive attitudes.

For Proctor, it was a change of nightmarish characteristics. He undoubtedly knew that all his achievements of the previous decade had come less easily to him than they would have to a white man. And he had to realize that his plans for the future were fraught with similar difficulty and uncertainty. But the events of 1841 and 1842 belied all his experience. Nothing in his past even hinted of this disaster and nothing prepared him to face it.

Although the $1,023 judgment on Nancy was smaller than the remainder of his adjudged debts, it was undoubtedly the most important. Still, those other debts bear investigation for what they reveal about Proctor and his society. Most of the cases were entered on the basis of Proctor's notes, commonly sums from $150 to $180, incurred between May 1840 and January 1841. The size of the notes and their frequency suggests that Proctor was either buying provisions for his family or seeking materials for the series of small construction projects he was involved in at that time. In any case, he made little or no attempt to contest the proceedings.[11]

The major suit of this series was *Asa Munson* v. *George Proctor*.[12] Munson was a miller on the south edge of Tallahassee. He owned his own lumberyard and mill, and at the beginning of 1840 he engaged Proctor for work there. Proctor built a

16 feet by 24 feet grist mill and enlarged or repaired the sawmill and a barn. Evidently the quality of Proctor's work was satisfactory, but Munson sued for the cost of materials he had supplied Proctor, a sum that Proctor thought excessive. In the end, however, they compromised on the figure of $840.09, although two months after the final decree, Proctor filed a countersuit against Munson for eight hundred dollars for his labor on the project.[13] The suit was eventually withdrawn, suggesting an out of court settlement that benefited Proctor.

But debts from these suits did not constitute the whole of the matter. While they were before the court, Proctor was struggling to pay off even larger debts that were just then coming due. It is reasonable to assume that he was successful in at least some cases, but in others he simply lacked sufficient resources to make good his obligations. The largest of these was a note for $882.31 for hiring the slave Pompey and had been endorsed to Thomas and Richard Hayward.[14] Plaintiffs sued for $1,600, but the court reduced the award to $1,038.42 in a decree of 17 November 1842. Three suits resulted in awards of $275 to $335. Two were for unpaid notes. One of these, *Flagg* v. *Proctor*, was, interestingly, originally from Proctor to Demilly, endorsed to DuVal and then endorsed to Francis Flagg, a local merchant.[15] The other was from Proctor to Salanthiel Crossman, a slater with whom Proctor had contracted for work in the past.[16] The third suit was *E.D. Coleman* v. *Proctor*, in which Proctor was to repay $275 worth of goods, services, or money (which one is unclear) by work.[17] Finally, four small suits resulted in awards of from $123 to $241.[18] Three of these were for notes given in 1839 and 1840, and the fourth was for hiring a Negro slave (Jack) in 1839.

Taken serially and in isolation, all but the Hayward award would have been bothersome but not serious for Proctor. But the combined effect, given his prior legal troubles, and the clear knowledge that he had struggled to pay off other notes, must have been devastating. It was hard to see how he could stave off Nancy's sale and utter ruin. And yet he did. The last of these awards came in 1843, and Proctor remained in Tallahassee until 1849; the family retained a measure of freedom until

1854. He was also able to satisfy all of these judgments except those of Hayward and Chandler, and he made progress on those. That Proctor achieved this much was a testament to his ability, his energy, and his friends. Certainly part of Proctor's success in staving off disaster was due to his legal aid. In many of the proceedings he was represented by counsel, most of the time by James Westcott, Jr.[19] Westcott was a man of talent and power; his identification as Proctor's attorney not only testified to Proctor's wisdom of maintaining friends among the powerful, it also undoubtedly gave him great aid in his legal battles. Although evidence is sketchy, it suggests that in the eight cases where Westcott represented Proctor, two were settled out of court, one was won, one was lost, and four were settled to Proctor's advantage. Proctor continued to use Westcott as his attorney until Westcott went to Washington in late 1845. The results are clear: in ordinary matters Proctor was treated as an equal of whites before the bench. And even though Proctor's real property was attached and sold, his family was never jeopardized as long as he remained in Tallahassee.

In three of the four damage suits that Proctor filed, Westcott was the attorney of record. One was the countersuit *Proctor v. Munson*, which was dismissed at plaintiff's consent on 16 December 1844.[20] Another was *Proctor v. Josiah Chaison*, a suit for an unpaid note to W.H. Francis that was endorsed to Proctor. In that proceeding Proctor was awarded $116.[21] A third suit was *Proctor v. Brown and Galbraith* where Proctor was represented by Thompson and Hogue who were often plaintiffs' attorneys in cases in which Proctor was defendant. In that suit Proctor won $274.[22] The fourth was *Proctor v. Henry Nichols' executor* where Proctor sued for $500 and was awarded $287, a case arising out of Proctor's work constructing a bake house. That case was not settled until 1849 when Westcott had been replaced by E.S. Dorsey.[23]

But the money Proctor gained from these suits was negligible: before 1845 it amounted to only $390, excluding what he may have gotten in the out of court settlement in his countersuit against Asa Munson. Despite that and Westcott's aid, the suits resulted in a debt of almost $5,500 against him by the end of 1843. This figure is staggering when compared with Proctor's resources. He obviously could not meet all the demands. In response, his creditors had his property seized. By the end of 1842 the sheriff had taken possession of and advertised for sale six of Proctor's city lots.[24] In the spring of 1842 the sheriff advertised the sale of Nancy and "sundry household and kitchen furniture—sideboard, looking glasses, beds and bedding, chairs, table, etc."[25] Even though the sale of Nancy did not occur, the advertisement testified to Proctor's predicament.

Ultimately only four of the lots were sold, for Proctor evidently did not hold clear title to the others. Those that were sold (30, 35, and 36 CQ and 167 OP) were all unimproved and brought only $491 toward the judgments against him. The other two (222 OP and 167 NA) were evidently lots where Proctor had built houses without holding clear title to the land. The land at 167 NA was the site of the Chaires mansion, which sold for $2,265 in late 1844, and 222 OP was the site of a small cottage valued at $1,600 in 1842. The price of 167 NA was probably fair market value or only slightly under, but the valuation of 222 OP, coming in the midst of the depression, is probably very low. In any case, if George built those houses—it seems clear that he did—it is fair to assume that his profit was in the range of eight hundred to a thousand dollars for the pair combined.[26] George had one obvious source of real income during these years—his buildings, though several of his projects were involved in the many suits he faced—the bake house for Henry Kingdon, the Munson gristmill, the work for Coleman, the project with Crossman, and the Chaires mansion.

His other projects included a 40 feet by 30 feet house with a slate roof built in 1841 and 1842 and the Randall-Lewis house.[27] The first is a mystery. It is at least possible that it was the Chaires house, which was constructed at that time and may have had a slate roof. If it was a separate structure, it was obviously a substantial one. If it and the Randall-Lewis house each brought Proctor profits of $800, a liberal estimate, that would have added another $1,600 to his income.

All of the income we know of or can estimate came to a

total of $3,500 on the most favorable account. This balanced against George's known debt of $5,500 left a shortfall of $2,000. Undoubtedly some debts and income are unknown to us, but it seems a fair assumption that these would approximately cancel each other out. Certainly large new debts would have appeared in court records, and significant income would have resulted in the debts of record being satisfied. There is but one kind of documentary evidence available to check these estimates. When Nancy and the children were sold in 1854, a final accounting was given. At that time George Proctor's debts were reckoned at $2,080, subject to minor credits.[28] Although this ought not be taken as explicit confirmation of the estimated two thousand dollar debt burden in 1845, still the closeness of the figures suggests that the figure was approximately correct.

Although George's debt burden was staggering, the surprising thing was his ability to pay as much of it as he did. Certainly that saved Nancy and the family. But with his legal and social handicaps, the wonderment at his achievement increases. Even given his friends in high places, his attorney, and his ability, the portion of his debt that he managed to pay still seems incredible. Only slightly less surprising is the realization that it was during this period of intense psychological and physical hardship that Proctor built two of his finest structures—the Chaires mansion and the Randall-Lewis house. The timing could have been more than coincidental. Both of these were large enough projects to produce a substantial profit. And, of course, Proctor needed the income not only to service his debts but to feed his family. As well, the Randall-Lewis house was constructed for Henry and Jane Rutgers, who would care for and protect the family in later years. Henry was a banker, and it is at least possible that there were dealings between Proctor and Rutgers this early and that the house was a kind of payment.

Then, just as Proctor finished these two fine structures, his work ceased, or at least what we know of his work ceased. From mid-1844 until he left Tallahassee in 1849, Proctor's building record was slight. The only substantial structure appears to have been the Rutgers house, done in late 1847 and early 1848. The reasons for this cessation are unclear. Certainly there are logical reasons why it may have occurred. It may very well have been that Proctor, with his debts, found it impossible to obtain the credit necessary to purchase materials: certainly he did not have the capital himself. Also, he may have found hardening pro-Southern and racial attitudes a barrier. Although the evidence suggests that most prominent and powerful Tallahasseeans regarded Proctor favorably, it is true that attitudes in the Deep South changed as the society drifted toward conflict. It is at least possible that these friendly Tallahasseeans may have come to regard Proctor's color as prohibiting his building trade even though they regarded his person as of old. Had this been the case, their pressure against his activity could have been anything from overt to very subtle, probably closer to the latter.

Finally, George may have experienced a problem with his will. Given the financial reverses and, more important, the social reverses, the change in status and the crushed hopes, George may have carried a psychological burden that prevented him from building. The circumstances appear to have been traumatic enough to produce that kind of wound. Proctor was intelligent and perceptive; his later life shows he was sensitive to such feelings or changes. Perhaps some combination of all of financial, social, and psychological factors prevented George from building after 1844.

Whatever the cause, George Proctor's Florida career as a builder effectively came to an end in the mid-1840s. He constructed one additional substantial house in Tallahassee in 1848, and he may have done some building in California, but his career was over in Tallahassee. Coming at mid-stride, this must have done its share of psychological damage as well. Limited possibilities were available to a free black man, and construction was at the top of the list. Then, too, with Judge Douglas's decree in effect so long as the mortgage on Nancy remained unsatisfied, George could not take his family out of Florida.

If George Proctor's world was not destroyed by the mid-1840s, its limits were certainly much restricted. Before then he—and to a large degree Tallahassee—were in many ways atypical of the Southern culture. But by the mid-1840s, that was no longer true. And as Tallahassee and Tallahasseeans matured and became committed to the Southern culture, Proctor found the resulting changes uniformly negative. Even if his friends wished to see his life unchanged, it would have taken immense personal courage and considerable coordination among them to accomplish it. There were obviously limits as to what could be expected of them. Indeed, that George's family remained secure and his movement within Florida not restricted seems proof that his friends stood by him through the crisis. In any case, George's period of ascent had ended.

FIVE

George's Defeat

Sometime in 1842 George Proctor moved his family out of the town of Tallahassee. It appears to have been a logical move; his construction business in Tallahassee was effectively finished. With the debts adjudged to him, he would probably have found it impossible to borrow money for his trade even if he had wanted to. He may have simply wanted to get out of the town where his troubles were and where his hopes and dreams had been dashed.

John Proctor said his father went to St. Marks—the nearest point on the Gulf Coast—"at one time to work on a wharf." [1] That certainly was within the realm of possibility. In the pre-railroad era the water route was the most economical for the movement of freight, and, as the economy rebounded in the mid-1840s, the need for able bodies would certainly have arisen at St. Marks. If George did find employment there, however, it did not last long.

Shortly after that time, George turned up living about one mile south of Tallahassee. There he rented twenty-five acres and a house from Benjamin Allen for a hundred dollars a year, the agreement to run for five years. [2] Allen and Proctor had known each other for some years. Allen, ten or fifteen years younger than George, was the son of Richard Allen, who had befriended and aided George earlier. Richard Allen died in the mid-1840s. Benjamin was a lawyer who served in both houses of the legislature in the late 1840s and, like his father, was a land speculator. Later in the 1850s, he would own and edit the *Sentinel*, the town's moderate, Whig newspaper.

As part of the bargain, Proctor was to make certain modifications to the structure and to farm the property. Evidently the new venture was partially successful, at least initially. By late 1846 Proctor and Allen had increased the scope of their agreement to include rental of Allen's slaves and an increase in the fee George was to pay. By this time George had expanded his operations to include growing corn and sea island cotton, neither of which was mentioned in the original agreement.[3]

The evidence suggests that George tried hard at farming. Indications are that he did little or no building or carpentry work for anyone but Allen between mid-1844 until at least mid-1846. The location of his residence and the expansion of his contract, moreover, indicate that he expended the major part of his effort on improving the farm. Farming in the mid-nineteenth century, after all, was not as far from a city boy's heart and knowledge as it would become a century later. Americans were still close to the soil, and it was an unusual male who could not make an honest attempt to support himself by husbandry should the need arise.

Throughout George's attempt at farming, however, ran the knowledge and consequences of his debt burden. He managed to extinguish much of the debt, but a significant portion remained—around two thousand dollars. He may have been able to make even further inroads on this sum, but there is no information as to the amount or the timing. It is unclear if there had been any payment on the Chandler account.[4]

The Chandler situation changed abruptly in 1846, and part of the change remains a mystery at a distance of a century and a half. In 1846 Mary Chandler remarried. The groom was a local widower, physician John B. Taylor. In reorganizing her personal affairs she either sold, transferred, or otherwise encumbered the execution on Nancy's mortgage. Whatever the circumstances, Mary Chandler did not own the execution by 1854: the execution itself was delivered to the sheriff 17 March 1846, shortly before the Chandler-Taylor union.[5] It is clear that whoever acquired the right to the execution was Proctor's friend, for it was never carried out while he was in Florida or for several years after.

Proctor's friends and benefactors did not desert him in his hour of need, but their exertions took a novel form. An attempt to return to the old patterns was impossible; it would have required an outright gift of money to reestablish Proctor's credit. And even that could not have influenced the hardening social and political situation. So George's friends resorted to an attempt to wipe out the debt with a coup: they applied to Congress for relief of Toney, George's father. But their motives were clearly to help George. During his long life, Toney had often served the government. He now claimed, in a sworn affidavit, that he was owed $1,600 for his services between 1822 and 1827. During that time he served as an Indian interpreter for Gad Humphries, Indian agent for the territory of Florida.[6] Although the official claim was not submitted until 1848, work on it began much earlier, probably in 1846. Then inquiries had gone off to Washington in Toney's name, trying to establish exactly what he had been paid and for what services.[7] By late 1847 the figuring was complete and a memorial went off to Congress with accompanying evidence.

The memorial is a testament to Toney's—and to some extent George's—position in society. It was signed by Governor Moseley, the secretary of state, the comptroller, the attorney general, and the presiding officers of both houses of the legislature in addition to thirty-seven members. Former governor DuVal appended his own positive recommendation. There was never any question that the Proctors occupied a special position in Florida, but this memorial in Toney's behalf and testifying to his character and services was an extraordinary, indeed spectacular, tribute to a black in a society drifting toward civil war in the name of slavery. Significantly, the memorial was introduced in the United States Senate by Senator James Westcott.

Toney by that time was over a hundred years old and had no obligations that are evident. He had not been party to any lawsuit and owned no property. It seems likely that he was being cared for by George or some other person and did not conduct his own affairs. George was the only Proctor with obligations, but he had no claim on the government or anyone else that would have been at all helpful. It is hard to see how any attempt for relief in his name would have proceeded with any possibility of success.

The claim for George in Toney's name goes far in explaining George's actions in the late 1840s. On the surface it appeared strong. Despite assurances of the auditor of the Treasury Department that records revealed substantial payments to Toney by Governor DuVal, DuVal signed the petition and sent his own supporting letter along with the memorial. Toney, DuVal agreed, had been paid, but not as much as his position justified. It was not an argument of gross neglect but one of injustice. As Leonard White has pointed out, this was a familiar kind of case—one in which "a sense of fairness and justice dictated relief, but where the strict rules of accounting officers prevented the normal process of settlement." Such cases were often settled favorably for the claimant, and, as White explains, Congress did spend much time and money settling the claims. Between 1834 and 1838, for example, Congress awarded $1,581,776.88 in such cases.[8] The claim's strongest feature, undoubtedly, was the list of persons supporting it. The elected governor, the state officers, and a substantial portion of the legislature lined up behind it. Its sponsor in Congress, while relatively new there, was familiar with the situation in Tallahassee and clearly sympathetic.

George must have had some hope that the claim would succeed. That hope or belief would go far toward explaining his situation during the period 1846-1849. Essentially, he was marking time on Benjamin Allen's farm. He may have had the knowledge and industry to farm, but twenty-five acres is testimony in itself that he was not going after agriculture as a road to salvation. The conclusion is that George went to the land while he waited to see what would happen. Were the claim successful, it would help wipe out his debts, which would remove the prohibition on Nancy leaving the state. Or, just as well, it might have opened the way for George to begin building again. But, if the claim were unsuccessful, it would clearly close the last door of escape.

The farming went sour. Despite initial success, by 1848 George found himself in trouble again. The cause is not known; it could have been anything from a natural disaster to bad management. But in July he acknowledged himself $450 in arrears to Allen for rent of land and slaves.[9] To escape the burgeoning debt, he pledged Allen a crop of corn in the field and sea island cotton seed as security, the money to fall due 1 January 1849. The debt was satisfied, although whether by crop or by cash is unknown. But, whatever the fact, the circumstances further suggest that farming was but a temporary expedient.

At about the same time, George began building again, in a very limited way. With the exception of the renovations and additions to Benjamin Allen's house, he had done no building since completing the Chaires mansion and the Randall-Lewis house in 1844. Then, in the summer of 1846, he contracted with the widow Eliza Ann Hobby for work on her fences and porches for which he was to receive $175. That work appears to have carried over until the fall or winter.[10] Then, sometime in the last half of 1847 or early 1848, he began work on the Rutgers house. There is no indication as to when Proctor and Henry Rutgers began to associate. It was obviously before 1842 when George began to work on the Randall-Lewis house for Rutgers. The relationship grew into something much closer than a simple business relationship. There was never any recorded contract between the two or, for that matter, any recorded paperwork at all, suggesting that very early theirs was a relationship based on trust. Given Rutgers's later actions and his position as banker, it is at least possible that Rutgers was loaning Proctor money—certainly he needed it then—and that the two houses Proctor built for him could have been a means to repay these debts or advances.[11]

Whatever the circumstances, Rutgers's county taxes and oral tradition in combination with this circumstantial evidence clearly establish the date and responsibility for the Rutgers house.[12] The construction probably lasted until mid-1848, by which time Proctor began his last Tallahassee home, one for John Maxwell at Bel Aire.[13] That project offers further evidence of Proctor's move back into building: the contracting party was not Proctor personally, but Geo. Proctor and Company.[14] That company included a partner, Jason Hart, but it was the existence of a company that was significant. It shows, first, that Proctor was probably operating under the hope of receiving money from the memorial to Toney: he was looking to the future with the new company. But the name indicated that he was still trading on his past: it was not Proctor and Hart, after all.

To confirm the renewed direction and motion came a newspaper advertisement in mid-1848 advertising "Moseley's Patent Sash Lock" for sale by George Proctor.[15] Common practice in that time was for such products to operate in a franchise-like system. That is, Proctor probably had sole rights to advertise and sell the device within the area. Taken together with Proctor and Company and with the Rutgers and Maxwell houses, it established Proctor's movement and mind-set. The experiment at farming was over; the debt to Allen had been settled.[16] He was still experiencing some negative forces. George lost his suit for damages against the Kingdons, and a judgment of $643 was made against him in 1848.[17] A third suit, *Proctor v. Nichols,* was settled out of court in 1849. The settlement is unknown at this distance, but it probably did not cost Proctor money and may have worked to his benefit.[18] With knowledge of the memorial's strengths and with hope ever present, Proctor must have expected the best. Were the memorial successful, the decade of the 1840s would have become merely a bad memory. The debts would have been cleared, and the burden on Nancy—and George—would have lifted.

But the memorial failed. The report of the Senate Committee on Indian Affairs, 25 January 1849, was adverse and without comment. The news must have reached Tallahassee quickly, and its effect would have been devastating. Like so many others of his generation, black and white, George Proctor was a victim. But he was black, and that fact made the situation damning. At no time would racial considerations be greater than in the fifteen years between the Mexican War and the Civil War. It was during that time that the Southern racial and sectional orthodoxy became absolute, and all vestiges of liberalism in the South disappeared. This meant not only that Proctor personally was doomed but that all the efforts of his white friends—rich and powerful though they might be— were destined to fail. Southern society could not admit so damning a contradiction as a successful free black.

News of the memorial's failure was the climactic end of Proctor's struggle in Tallahassee. Within two months he had made his decision to leave Florida and his family. Clearer indication of the impact of the news was not needed. Tallahassee was all he knew, and his family was all that he had. Given his faith in purchasing and marrying Nancy, the size of his family, and his attempt to stay with and support them over the previous decade, leaving them was a complete reversal. Likewise, for all the hardship and changing attitudes he had faced in Tallahassee, it also contained all of his friends and sponsors. Giving up this protection must have been an intensely difficult decision, brought on only by the realization of the ultimate hopelessness of his situation.

At any rate, a brief notice appeared in the *Floridian*, 10 March 1849. "In bidding adieu to my friends and patrons, I would return them my most sincere thanks and heartfelt gratitude for the kindness, liberality and patronage extended to me from the days of my boyhood to the present. George Proctor." [19] The tone of the notice was positive, but the sentiments it stood for were devastating: it expressed the helplessness of the Southern situation.

The notice also offered continuing confirmation of Proctor's status with his patrons. Despite his failures and the heightening racism of the time, he still had the confidence and trust of white social and political leaders. He was black, his wife and children were slaves, he owed a great amount of money, but he was able to leave Florida on a hazardous journey without undue jeopardy to himself or his family. The plan, obviously, was not for a permanent separation. Proctor undoubtedly planned to go west to seek—and make—his fortune. Perhaps he planned to look for gold, although the California record gives scant evidence of that. More than likely he planned to follow the only trades he knew: carpentry and land speculation. Clearly there would be a need for builders and land speculation was bound to be rife.

Two other considerations may have influenced George. First, California, then a territory, was obviously going to be a free state. It was clear that racial prejudice and perhaps some civil disabilities would accompany the new population to California, but slavery would not. That would have been very important to George Proctor. Second, the California he emigrated to would be much like the Tallahassee of the 1830s—a fluid, flexible frontier community, the kind of community in which the Proctors had found their greatest successes. It was only natural that George should seek out such a place. There may have been no explicit recognition on his part that he sought a similar frontier community. But surely some unconscious intuition moved him in that direction, for it was unlike him to strike out blindly.

On a different level, news of the gold strike inflamed all Americans' imaginations. As one perceptive student put it: "there was something unreal, storybookish," about the gold rush, producing "a sudden and overwhelming response." Many, perhaps most, of the men who rushed to California "were like the dust devils, whirling hither and yon in search of a destiny they rarely contemplated and never wholly understood." The odds in favor of finding gold—or riches of any kind—were desperately long, but the opportunity created intense excitement.[20] George Proctor was not one of those who ignored or misunderstood the forces that governed his life, but he could not have been immune to the California excitement. Other prominent and otherwise sober Tallahasseeans were not: gold fever had the same impact in the Florida capital that it had throughout the United States. Almost everyone talked about the gold rush, and some broke loose and went to California—some like dust devils and some infinitely more serious— to seek riches of one kind or another.

News of the gold strike was well known in Tallahassee and north Florida; George Proctor was not the only one to succumb to its allure. Several others, in better material and mental circumstances than George, decided to "seek their fortunes in this new land of promise," as one local report put it. One party included Thomas Hayward, a prominent merchant and one of Proctor's creditors; George McMullin, established merchant; two Maxwells of the locally prominent family; and Washington Bartlett, newspaper editor, grandnephew of the Declaration of Independence signer Josiah Bartlett, and future mayor of San Francisco and governor of California.[21] Seen beside these men, Proctor's aspirations seem respectable and solid. (Bartlett and Proctor, by the way, were probably more than simply acquaintances, although not close enough for Proctor to accompany the Bartlett party. Proctor had advertised in Bartlett's *Star of Florida* in the past, and Bartlett's social and political ideas were certainly compatible with such a friendship.)

The decision to go to California must have been made quickly, and preparations for the departure proceeded apace. Business arrangements remain mysterious. Proctor may have had a cash reserve, but that seems doubtful. More likely he borrowed money from Rutgers. At least there is an extant check for three hundred dollars from Proctor to Rutgers that was cashed after Proctor had left Tallahassee. That is also the figure that gained currency as the proper funding required for the trip.[22] George had one final lawsuit to fight: *Proctor and Company v. John P. Maxwell* for the six hundred dollars George sought for building Maxwell's house at Bel Aire. That suit was filed after George left Tallahassee, and the award barely sufficed to pay Henry Rutgers his three hundred dollars.[23] Most of the preparations George made remain unknown. It is significant that on 4 March 1849 the last three Proctor children, Mahainem Stewart, Mary Magdaline, and George, were baptized at St. John's.[24]

George probably left the following week, going first to New Orleans and then by boat to San Francisco. He did not intend to come back to Florida, but rather to have his family join him elsewhere once he was secure and could satisfy the mortgage on Nancy. But he never did return to Tallahassee, and his family never joined him. They never saw him again. And in poignant commentary on the Proctors and the Southern way of life, while Proctor was seeking to buttress their freedom, white Tallahassee would sell Nancy and the children to satisfy George's debts.

SIX

California

Arrangements complete and affairs in order, George Proctor left Tallahassee for St. Marks. There he took the regular packet ship for New Orleans, a favorite embarkation point for forty-niners. He left New Orleans on 17 April 1849 bound for San Francisco via Chagres on the bark *Florida*. The ship was a small one, evidently in good condition, and its route was known as the quickest. Once committed, evidently, Proctor wanted no delays.[1]

His quest was not a unique one. Rudolph Lapp points out that "the gold mines of California . . . had a powerful attraction for black men," who saw in this gamble a chance worth taking. Some, he explains, "left wives and children behind as hostages" and "others who were already free hoped to buy freedom for their families." For those who had the luxury of choice, "the water route suggested greater personal security than did the land routes."[2]

Even if George's quest was not unique, that did not make it any less lonely or climactic. He struck off, evidently by himself, with all the inherent disabilities and dangers that his color brought with it. It must have been terrifying; it was unlike anything he had ever known. His removal to Tallahassee had been protected by friends and sponsors in high places, and it had been a move within a familiar society. His father's name and reputation had preceded him and, in many ways, protected him and guaranteed his chances. None of those factors operated in George's move to California. Friends, fame, and familiarity had been left behind. Yet in another sense, it was a return to a familiar situation. Antonio had succeeded in fluid, changing St. Augustine. Now, California was the fluid, changing location, as Tallahassee had been in the 1830s. And with a new, diverse population like the one George had found in early Tallahassee, California offered him the kind of world where he had done best.[3] Then, of course, there was the lure of gold.

It is unclear whether or not George went to California to find gold. That was the great hope for most who went, but there were some who had other things in mind. When Washington Bartlett left Tallahassee, for example, he took with him a printing press, obviously looking forward to publishing rather than prospecting on the West Coast. Proctor was a skilled tradesman, and he was intelligent enough to understand the odds against a given individual finding gold. One could argue that he intended to follow his trade of building and land speculation in California. Rudolph Lapp concludes that among the blacks who went to California were those who were not gold seekers but men who were determined to make their living by the skills they took with them.[4]

The first hint of George in California suggests that this may have been his design. In June 1849 a firm identified only as "Proctor and Co." was recorded as having "made the first settlement and improvement upon the 'Green Springs Rancho.'" In October that year "Proctor and Co." sold the improved property for three thousand dollars.[5] That "Proctor and Co." may not have been George, but surviving documents suggest no other Proctors in the area at the time. More to the point, Green Springs was on the line of travel between San Francisco and the prime gold country, and it was precisely the kind of activity that Proctor knew best—land speculation and building. It is entirely reasonable to assume, given the surviving documents and knowledge of his personal history, that George Proctor, with a small crew he picked up and probably with some financial backing, was responsible for the Green Springs Rancho. The increased value of the land with buildings on it, and the accompanying price inflation would have meant that he derived substantial profit from the venture, certainly enough to stake him in the gold country itself.

If it was George Proctor who built the Green Springs Rancho, it provided him with an auspicious start in that new country. It also would have served to suggest to him that his old skills and experience might prove more useful than looking for gold. In this instance it is important to point out that there is no known record—public or private—to suggest that he ever prospected or engaged in any significant mining activity. From what is known of Proctor's movements, the timing for the Green Springs project also works well. The first explicit notice of him is in Sonora on 20 January 1851 in a property transaction. By that time he had acquired a partner and, obviously, some knowledge of local conditions, suggesting he had not just arrived. In other words, Proctor may have left Green Springs in late 1849 with some money in his pocket and within the next year established himself in Sonora.

Sonora, the county seat of Tuolumne County, was built in the heart of the gold country. Originally settled in 1848 by Mexicans from the state of Sonora, it retained a substantial Spanish population until 1851. At that time the new, American settlers imposed a tax on noncitizens, which succeeded in driving the Mexicans out. Strikes of gold were commonplace and appear to have been unusually large, which, of course, served to draw more prospectors and settlers to the area.[6]

Enos Christman, who settled in the town and for a time edited the Sonora *Herald*, left the best brief description of the town and its inhabitants: "Sonora is a fast place and make no mistake. Such a motley collection as we have here can be found nowhere but in California. Sonora has a population hailing from every hold and corner of the globe—Kanakas, Peruvians, Negroes, Spaniards, Mexicans, Chileans, Chinese, British convicts from New South Wales, known as "Sidney Birds," Englishmen, Frenchmen, Dutch, Paddies, and not a small sprinkling of Yankees. We have more gamblers, more drunkards, more ugly, bad women, and larger lumps of gold, and more of them, than any other place of similar dimension within Uncle Sam's dominions. The Sabbath is regarded as a holiday, granting men and women more extensive license to practice vice than any other day of the week."[7] The resemblance to early Tallahassee is striking. The diverse population, "anarchy and excitement," rapidly increasing population, and the concept of growth and change must have made for a sense of déjà vu in the transported Tallahasseean. George must have sensed the difference, though: the lack of family and patrons. But the sense of isolation was probably less bothersome than it might appear at first glance. George was now a mature forty-four years old and not the mere boy-apprentice who had gone to Tallahassee. The obvious economic activity must have provided some compensation.

It was, undoubtedly, the kind of situation that would enable George to regain a sense of optimism and energy. At any rate, he plunged immediately into the midst of the new cosmos. His first moves, evidently, were in finding friends and partners, the concept of patrons and sponsors being, for the moment at least, out of the question. Proctor initially lived with George Work, the county sheriff, who was white. This may have been as close to the familiar sponsor/patron concept as Proctor could get and recalls his relationship with Romeo Lewis, the sheriff of Leon County. Regardless, it was not a bad move, associating him in at least some degree with the local power structure. At the same time he found a partner of sorts in Emanuel Villalonga, who had lived at the Algerine Camp, known as "one of the richest, rowdiest, and most bloodthirsty places" in the area.[8]

It is unclear how long George remained close to either Work or Villalonga. The suggestion is that both relationships were brief, evidently lasting only until he was able to establish himself. Certainly the Spanish influence waned swiftly, and Work was killed in the line of duty shortly thereafter.

In January 1851 Proctor and Villalonga purchased the Florida House on North Washington Street, the town's primary commercial artery. The Florida House was an established business, certainly not the town's major hotel but clearly a recognized establishment. It was evidently small (the lot measured 36 feet of frontage on Washington Street, and its depth was 100 feet); the price was but eight hundred dollars.[9] The financial details are murky. No cash changed hands. Proctor and Villalonga agreed to make good the price in four installments of two hundred dollars each, beginning in March and to be completed in June of that year.[10] It is revealing that, if Proctor did build and profit from the Green Springs Rancho, he did not use the cash to acquire the Florida House outright. The knowledge that he had acquired a partner gives the question more importance. Most likely he was making investments for future gain. Such behavior was, after all, what he knew.

The facts are clear. He was sending money to Tallahassee, though how much is unknown.[11] He was acquiring other properties—when and for how much is unknown, although absence of recorded mortgages suggests that he paid cash for them.[12] And, given the time and place, he could have been backing mining ventures, although there is no documentary evidence of this. From all this evidence, it seems George Proctor was not working solely to send every penny he made to Florida. His goal, clearly, was to invest for larger gains. Whether his object was to settle the Florida obligations rapidly and quickly reunite the family or to realize his entrepreneurial dream and have his family will never be accurately known, but the course seems evident.

George and his partner were evidently able to satisfy the payments of the Florida House. The purchase and operation of the establishment fit well with Proctor's background and with the California experience. "Some blacks," Rudolph Lapp notes, "set up their own boarding houses and eateries. . . . a black man could be fairly certain of his self-respect in a black operated" establishment.[13] Proctor had experience in business operation and, especially, in land speculation. The Florida House was in a good location, although there was stiff competition for businesses like that in Sonora. It had been in operation for at least eleven months prior to Proctor's acquisition. He and his partner seem to have entrusted its management to H.H. Nichols, an experienced and respected manager of such enterprises, perhaps even making him a third partner in ownership. Given Proctor's lack of familiarity with hotel management and a seeming lack of familiarity from Villalonga, this must have been a wise move. Nichols, like Proctor, was black.[14] Florida House remained the mainstay of Proctor's operations in Sonora throughout 1851 and 1852 and perhaps 1853. He twice borrowed money using the property for security, once for five hundred dollars and once for a thousand dollars.[15] Both mortgages were satisfied on schedule. At some point he acquired at least four other pieces of property containing seven tenant houses—one, at least, occupied by Chinese.[16] The acquisition of these properties is unrecorded in the official records, suggesting that the records did not note all transactions that took place. Then in late 1852 George bought out his partner, Emanuel Villalonga.

By 1852, George Proctor appeared to have made a promising start in California. The county tax roll that year assessed him for property worth nine hundred dollars, although it did not indicate whether it was real or personal property. His standing and attitude is further shown by a newspaper account that a petition from Proctor had been referred to a committee of the Sonora council.[17] Although knowledge of the petition's contents have not survived, the important fact is that Proctor felt well placed enough to petition the council and that the council felt Proctor was substantial enough to consider the matter. Proctor also had acquired and was operating a recognized and respectable business and had established his credit and reputation with prominent white citizens of Sonora.

The risky venture showed promise. Against heavy odds, Proctor seemed to have regained the initiative in his struggle with the world. The entrepreneurial dream that had been choked in Tallahassee blossomed fully in Sonora. The goals businessman Proctor had adopted in the late 1830s were attained in the early 1850s. The overwhelming impression, borne out by documentary evidence, is that George Proctor was an aggressive, successful member—albeit a black one—of the town's business community.

But the promise was not to continue. On 18 June 1852, Sonora burned. The *Herald* described it well: "The calamity that has been so long feared has at length come upon us.

Sonora, the chief city of the Southern mines, which has for so long a time enjoyed impunity, while conflagration was raging all over the country, is at length laid in ruins. . . . all, all is gone." In the list of losses that followed, George Proctor was shown to have had two thousand dollars' worth of his property destroyed.[18]

George must have found this all very familiar. His promising beginning, his new career and hopes for his family, had been dashed. Fire was the omnipresent, universally-feared calamity in all wooden frontier villages, and there was no real protection from it. Proctor had seen it happen in 1843 Tallahassee, although he evidently suffered no loss. Now this fire hurt him severely. For all his success, Proctor could not have been expected to overcome his loss. It seems clear he had no liquid assets—all those would have been going to Tallahassee—and that he had heavily invested in income-producing property. Insurance was out of the question. In addition, Proctor probably had personal notes outstanding—although they were unrecorded—at the time of the fire. Now, with his income undoubtedly greatly reduced, he was still liable for his debts. Whether the Florida House was destroyed, damaged, or untouched by the fire's path is unclear, but notice of the building—or its successor—appears again in December 1852.

By October Proctor was being sued for $543.42, and in December the Florida House was attached to satisfy the judgment.[19] Unknown, of course, is whether or not Proctor had other contemporary debts that he managed to satisfy. In some manner, he evidently managed to pay—or postpone—this $543.42 note, for the sale of the Florida House did not take place at that time.

But in March 1853 came another suit against Proctor and Villalonga, this time resulting in an award of $2,624 to the plaintiff William Reynolds. The Florida House was sold to satisfy the debt. Although it brought nowhere near the amount of the award,[20] it seems to have satisfied Proctor's liability in the case. There are no other recorded court actions against him until late 1853.

In fact, recorded notice of Proctor does not exist at all

between 1853 and 1859. It seems most likely that he remained in the area of Sonora.[21] Certainly the destruction from the fire would have left him opportunities to ply his trade of building. Perhaps he tried mining. From later indications, he retained the respect of the community throughout this period.

So it was failure again for George. The fire had severely damaged his dream, and his options were limited and unattractive. Little, obviously, was to be gained by returning to Tallahassee—assuming he had the cash reserves necessary for the trip. He did not have the means to satisfy his obligations in Florida, and with the nation drifting to Civil War, it was clear that social and racial attitudes there would have hardened rather than relaxed. The Florida option, thus, was not appealing. The alternative was to stay in California. His immediate obligations evidently had been satisfied, so there was no pressure—or danger—from that quarter. If he was indeed following his trade, he must have found opportunity for work and income produced both by the destructiveness of the fire and by the growing population. And, of course, Sonora continued to produce large quantities of gold throughout the decade and into the 1860s.[22] Staying in the West, while not necessarily promising, must have seemed the more reasonable to George. Return to Florida would have reunited him with his family but in most discouraging circumstances. Remaining in California meant continued separation from Nancy and the children, but it held at least some promise, however small, of ultimate success. And, of course, it is only the advantage of hindsight that suggests the lack of promise that course held.

George communicated with his family in Florida. He received letters in Sonora, although the point of origin of the correspondence is unknown.[23] Oral tradition is explicit that his family received letters from him. (One version concluded that of these, Nancy "was allowed to receive only one letter, which she was forced to surrender."[24]) He would have had to explain why he stopped sending money, and there is no reason to expect he would not have explained the reasons. His change in fortune would have been known in his former home.

George soon learned of a tragedy in Tallahassee, one even

greater than the one in Sonora. As with most events concerning the Proctors, the event is surrounded by mystery. The hard fact, however, was clear. On 6 February 1854, Nancy and the six children were sold at auction.[25] The fire that severely impeded George's chances of financial success in California must have removed any faith his creditors in Florida retained—and there had been two years for judgment between the fire and the sale.

The next year Toney died. He was vigorous to the last. His eyesight had dimmed, and his memory was at times uncertain, but his health and spirit were strong. On 18 June 1855, on being asked how he felt, however, he replied, "Ah Ben, I'm going." He died that day.[26]

How much did George know of the events in Tallahassee? The answer is unclear. A "gentleman" in Sonora who knew George well asserted that "Proctor wrote repeatedly to his old home but never got an answer; and finally gave it up."[27] That may be. But other statements in the document suggest that there was more direct and complete knowledge than Proctor may have wanted to admit. Whether guilt and shame made him admit only sketchy knowledge or if that was truly all he knew, the fact is that Proctor knew enough of the story to understand what had happened to his family. The news must have been the greatest shock in his life. It defined, better than any other event in his life had, the condition of his society and raised ultimate questions about his character. He never paid for Nancy despite an income that was at times substantial, he may have owned slaves, and he obviously leased and used slaves. And the facts are clear: he abandoned Nancy and the children in Tallahassee, and he did not come back—even after learning of the tragedy.

The actions can be logically explained. He did not pay for Nancy at the time because he lacked cash, and, besides, it was the way George the entrepreneur purchased everything else; it had always worked before. More damning is the knowledge that even when he was earning money after the panic of 1837 he paid other debts rather than satisfying the mortgage on his wife. Why? The only answer is that he was convinced that Tallahassee would not violate the sanctity of his marriage and

family, an understanding with Mary Chandler (Taylor) and her
successor to the debt, and an optimistic belief that he would
pay all debts, either through success of the congressional petition or a return of good times. Material success was obviously
of great importance to him, and it was the only way to free his
family.

There is legal documentation that the Chandler debt, regardless of who owned it, took precedence over all others in the
eyes of the court.[28] An understanding with Chandler or the
execution holder to permit payment of other debts first would
have explained why his earnings did not go to satisfy the
mortgage on Nancy.

The slaveholding question is impossible to resolve; more
to the point is the realization that even if he did not own
slaves, he was a part of the slaveholding system when he
leased bondsmen from others or sublet them to whites. Mor-
ally damning? Without question. His treatment of the slaves
is unknown, and his attitude toward the practice at that time
is unspoken. Even with the knowledge that there was probably no other way he could find a work crew, the answer to the
slaveholding question puts Proctor in moral jeopardy and
confirms his devotion to the American middle-class dream of
material success.

He did leave Nancy, his children, and his father in Tallahassee. It is hard to see how he could have done otherwise, and, as
Lapp has observed, others were forced by circumstances to do
the same. Toney was ancient, and a court order prevented
Nancy from leaving Florida. It seems clear that George believed he had guaranteed their immediate safety with powerful friends in Tallahassee. By that time, it probably had seemed
the only recourse he had. Certainly his situation in the late
forties, especially after the petition failed, was not encourag-
ing. He could have returned in the mid-1850s. Even with the
drift toward civil war, conditions were such that the journey
would have been physically possible for him, and he did not
know that the war was coming. To have purchased his family's
freedom would have shut the door on the possibility of an

economic miracle, but it would have reunited husband, wife, and children.

Any judgments are speculative, but some are logical. George was of special status, and he acted as though he knew it throughout his life. He pleaded in court as a white; he was taxed as a white; his family was accorded the sanctity of a white family. He may have been so blinded by this special status of his that he failed to understand the dangers confronting him. That counts as naïveté and as a serious blunder.

Ignoring the odds, George ultimately placed his reliance on business success rather than accepting his second-class status. His early life was a model of typically frontier American values and practices. The California odyssey represented an attempt at the big strike; the time for incremental gains was over. Certainly his hardships were both cruel and intense. Certainly many otherwise sober middle-class Americans were caught up in the California fever, but for Proctor it represented a major weakness: he ignored the lessons of his early career, threw caution to the winds, and failed. George had fifteen years left him and more pain to come. Nancy remarried, and there is every reason to believe that George knew of it. Now his ruin was complete.

George appears to have spent the rest of his life in Sonora. He does not appear in the 1860 census there, but other evidence places him in the town.[29] In many ways, however, his life, at least as he had known and dreamed of it, ended in the mid-1850s. Even if the dream of material success did not disappear, the reality of his catastrophe in the early 1850s must have dimmed it. And with that catastrophe, knowledge of the 1854 sale in Tallahassee, and the final blow of the late 1850s—the dissolution of his marriage—his dream disappeared. For above all else, George Proctor was no fool: his experiences had shown him the difference between reality and fantasy.

In the remaining years of his life, indeed until the very end, George Proctor adopted a new dream. That is not to suggest that it necessarily replaced his old dreams, but his life led him to a new goal: civil rights for his race. A friend in Sonora

believed that there was an obvious cause and effect relationship between George's older and newer dreams. It was the
tragedy in Tallahassee that produced his "zeal" in the cause of
freedom for his color.[30]
    George was not alone in this work. In this new California
was a large segment of the population devoted to the advancement of black rights. It was only natural that such a movement
would appear, for the California dream was bound to attract
forceful, vigorous persons who looked to the future. The course
of history by that time was in the direction of black advancement—witness the rapid onset of the Civil War—and many
blacks and whites who came to the new state were fervent in
their determination that it be achieved there. Also, needless to
say, a sizable part of the population were determined to prevent such advancement.[31] The movement for black rights had
determined advocates in Tuolumne County. Rudolph Lapp,
who explored that movement with clarity and completeness,
notes that it revolved around two goals: civil rights and education.[32] Although blacks did not achieve their aims until after
his death, the struggle was well advanced during his lifetime,
and George was an active participant. He was listed as the
Sonora agent for the *San Francisco Elevator,* prime mover in
the cause.[33]
    Fourteen months before his death, he produced a par-
ticularly articulate and forceful letter in the *Elevator.*[34] We
have no reason to believe that the letter and the sentiments it
contained are not his own. He was literate, he was known to be
a participant in the cause, and the events of his life could not
have helped but produce the sentiments the letter expounded.
It addressed the issues in view of a new petition praying for
black suffrage to be presented to the California legislature.
Tuolumne citizens of "African descent," Proctor proclaimed,
viewed the petition as "impolitic and unwise." While they were
anxious to have the ballot, he said, "they do not feel like acting
the part of the whipped spaniel, by turning around and licking
the hand of the party which had forged their chains in times
past" and who opposed the petition itself. Instead, Proctor
implored, "let us be men and show . . . that we would sooner

wait and combat the popular prejudice until more liberal views shall prevail." He did not wish to see blacks "whiningly" beg for "that boon from the now dominant party." [35] "Let us be men," he counseled. If anyone was justified in shouting those words, it was George Proctor. Defeated at every turn, undoubtedly burdened by incredible guilt at the events his submission to established society had brought, this sixty-two-year-old man had reached his limit. Now he fought not only for the memory of his family and his personal salvation but for all people of his color.

Although civil rights activities were new ones for Proctor, his more mundane activities during the last years of his life were very familiar. By then identified as a miner and carpenter, he seems to have carried on his trade in a straightforward manner.[36] In September 1859 he was in court for nonpayment of a note and lost the case (for $128.89) by default.[37] Then, in 1861, he was again sued for debt, and as a result had his last four recorded properties seized and sold by the county to pay for the execution. These parcels were his last income-producing structures, including his own residence at the corner of Shepard and Lyons streets.[38] Evidently he owned no real property in the county after that time.

In the last recorded incident of George's life, in mid-1862 he was sued for $57.80 and possession of Zion's Chapel, identified as a "colored Church." Plaintiff was the chapel itself, represented by its trustees. The surviving records of the case are incomplete, but evidently Proctor held the real property against the will of the trustees. The case was decided against him, and he quickly paid the sum and gave up his hold on the property.[39]

From that point until his death, George disappears from the record. He evidently carried on for the five remaining years as before, supporting himself by his trade and maintaining his activities in the cause of black advancement. It is worth noting that there is some negative evidence about his activities. There are no mining claims in his name, suggesting that whatever mining he was doing was either as a laborer or on a very small scale, and, of course, he never made a strike. Significantly, there is no evidence that he married in California; he remained faithful to the memory of Nancy and his family.[40]

Last mention of George Proctor came in two places: the Sonora City Cemetery Burial Record and in his obituary in the *San Francisco Elevator.* The burial record shows his death on 28 December at age 64 and lists the reason as consumption. He was buried in grave #198 in a section of the cemetery that has fallen into neglect with burial sites indistinct and markers missing. His obituary gave the date of his passing as 26 December and his age as sixty-three years, eight months, and three days, identifying him as an "old resident of Sonora where he has lived since 1850 and was highly respected by all who knew him."[41]

So George Proctor failed. To have expected otherwise would have been to expect the impossible—or at least the highly improbable. He had intelligence, spirit, ancestry, and a trade. But these characteristics were not enough to overcome his color and his time or, as the case may be, his flaws. Success—even without the flaws—would have required luck, and that he could not produce by himself. The failure, moreover, was absolute. He lost his wife, his family, his property, and he died in a strange place. Today his grave is unmarked. It is hard to imagine a worse end. But the tragedy of George Proctor was also the tragedy of his society.

SEVEN

George's Family

At George Proctor's departure the family unit was intact and would remain so for a decade. Toney the patriarch was ninety-nine and, for his age, active and lucid. Nancy, thirty-four, had five of the surviving children in her care: Charlotte, age nine; Georgianna, age six; John, who had accompanied his father to St. Marks for his departure, age four; Mahainam Stewart, three years old; and George, the baby, who was one. A sixth child, Mary, who would have been three years old, appears to have survived but evidently was not with the family in 1850. The final member of the household was George's cousin Lydia Stout, later Smith, age twenty-nine.[1]

Nancy does not appear to have been a strong, dominant personality, which is not to judge her role as a nurturer or as a mother. Nowhere does any picture of her personality appear. None of the children, significantly, with the possible exception of Georgianna and Mary who—probably because of marriage—disappear from view, named any of their children after Nancy.[2]

Lydia Stout was a free mulatto: her presence in the house was ambiguous. If George had understood that Nancy might require help in his absence, it would aid in explaining Lydia Stout's presence. John remembered that his father had "persuaded" Lydia to come to Tallahassee "to be a governess" for the children. John also remembered that Lydia was from the Bahamas, although she told the census takers that she had been born in Florida. A substantial person in her own right, Lydia would marry the Methodist pastor James Smith. She became a school teacher and was a pillar of the black community throughout her life.[3]

At the time of his departure, the entire family was probably legally considered the slave property of George, even though they were recorded as being free in the 1850 census. The location of the household is unclear. While the family would be under the care—and ownership—of the Rutgerses later in the decade, in 1850 they appear to have been residing in the country, and the Rutgerses remained in town.[4]

As the bonds of slaves became critically important to Southerners, and without George and his connections to the power structure, the family's situation grew precarious. It is unlikely, though, that their sale was routine; some critical event must have precipitated the act. The sheriff had received the execution in 1846, three years before George departed, and he had held it for four years.

The most likely conclusion is that news of the Sonora disaster arrived, and the money from George stopped coming. George was making money until the fire, and he was sending a portion of it back to Tallahassee. But after the fire and the large adverse judgment that resulted in the sale of the Floiida House a year later, it is hard to conceive how the payments to Tallahassee could have continued. The sale of the family occurred early in February 1854.

Proctor had left the family with a person he thought would protect them in all circumstances. A "gentleman" in Sonora explained that Proctor had "left the family's papers with a lawyer in whom he had the utmost confidence." John explicitly named James Archer as being this person. Archer, who was Florida's first secretary of state, was an attorney active in business. Among other things he was one of the trustees for Henry Rutgers's South Western Railroad Bank bond. But no legal documentation confirms John's identification of him as the execution's holder. There is, in fact, no other evidence of any connection between George Proctor and James Archer.[5] In the same conversation, John identified Henry Rutgers as being his father's "agent." This helps to explain Benjamin Allen's statement that Henry Rutgers was "in charge" of the family, a fact confirmed by the legal record that noted at the time of the sale that the Proctors were in "possession" of Rutgers.[6]

It is unclear how Archer acquired the Chandler execution. Likewise, the nature of the relationship between Archer and Proctor remains unknown, although Archer did sign the petition to Congress for Toney's relief. Only the timing, in fact, suggests that Allen's holding the execution was not wholly a humanitarian gesture. Coming so soon after Proctor's California disaster, the family's sale indicates some degree of economic motivation in Archer's action. The alternative is to suggest that George Proctor misjudged his man.

Nancy and the six children were sold to Jane Rutgers apart from her husband Henry. This move must have been designed to protect them from being caught up in Henry Rutgers's business dealings. Although he was a member of the bar, by trade Rutgers was a banker—none too stable a profession in Florida. He was associated with the local Union Bank in Tallahassee and was the agent for the South Western Railroad Bank of Charleston. His personal affairs, unfortunately because of performance bonds he maintained, were entwined with the fortunes of both institutions.

Tallahassee banks, as all southern and western banks, were heavily dependent on northeastern capital and credit for normal operations. As the banks in that region began to anticipate the hard times that would become the panic of 1857, the ripples had impact in Tallahassee. Rutgers felt them as waves. In January he mortgaged everything—personal property, house, and slaves, except the Proctors—as part of his bond. By late summer he was forced to borrow again, this time mortgaging the Proctors too. He found ways to satisfy both obligations the next year but shortly afterward went to the well again and mortgaged three of the children for cash.[7]

The breakup of the family came soon after and was coincident with the breakup of the Union. Robert Williams briefly gained custody of John and Bahamia. John quickly became the property of Matthew Lively and Bahamia was sold to the

Finlayson family in Jefferson County. Georgianna went to a Mr. Fernando. Charlotte, Mary, and George were sold at a price of $2,800 to George W. Scott at the beginning of 1860. Scott was a Tallahassee merchant and would become a noted cavalry commander during the war. Following the conflict, he was the Democratic candidate for governor in 1868. After leaving Tallahassee in the early 1870s he made a substantial mark in Georgia and later founded the college named after his daughter Agnes in Atlanta. By all accounts he was an intelligent, sensitive, and humane person.[8]

Nancy's course was surprising: she married the black minister Samuel Wells. The circumstances are unknown, but by 1866 she was known as Nancy Wells, and the couple evidently produced a child, Henrietta, in 1858. Fragmentary evidence suggests that the Wells family lived in close proximity to the Scotts and that all members of the Proctor family remained in close contact.[9]

Florida remained in the Union long enough for the federal census to be completed. This time the Proctors were considered slaves and, for that reason, not recorded in the document. Scott's household had no slaves whose ages fit those of Charlotte, Mary, and George, suggesting that they had been enumerated as part of his plantation slave stock. The Rutgerses, likewise, showed no slaves in their household, and, since they owned no plantation, the suggestion is that the other Proctors may have been sold, or lost by mortgage foreclosure, to some unnamed owner. Lydia Stout, revealingly, was enumerated as the head of a household with two black males, Jack Hall, a farm laborer, and Jason Hart, George Proctor's erstwhile business partner. They appear to have lived near the Rutgers homestead on North Calhoun Street.[10]

Henry Rutgers died the next year. Abruptly following the settlement of the estate—which does not mention the Proctors—all mention of his widow and his brother ceases in the records. Evidently they left the town.

By this time the war had begun. It was hard on Tallahassee and its citizens. No battles were fought there; the event celebrated in the town as the Battle of Natural Bridge occurred in the last months of the war and was no more than a skirmish. But military affairs aside, the impact was great. Not only were many males in uniform—and for the most part out of Florida since there was little action there—the economic impact was considerable. Commerce stagnated. With Northern markets gone and the blockade in place, cotton provided no profit, and, for the same reason, store shelves emptied of goods from outside the South. By the end of 1863 the *Sentinel* stopped publication because newsprint was unavailable. War's end brought no relief. In December 1865 the city council borrowed money to meet expenses. Other harsh realities soon intruded as Federal troops came in numbers and confiscated a Monroe Street store and other buildings around town for army use.

When the war came John Proctor was seventeen. It is difficult to follow him, although in his dotage he insisted he had pleasant memories of the time.[11] John had great respect and affection for Henry Rutgers and after his death searched for other surrogate figures to fill this second loss. Three men, all whites from substantial families, filled the need in some measure. Willy Ames, the railroad depot agent, taught him to read and write. B.C. Lewis, who would become the town's banker, taught him math. John remembered Mr. Lewis drawing pictures to explain the multiplication tables. But it was Matthew Lively who provided the most guidance and sustenance for John. He was also John's owner. Lively was half-owner of the Ames and Lively drug store. John worked in the store as a clerk; he appears to have performed the full range of duties expected of such persons.[12]

John retained affection and respect for Lively all his life. He voted him aid as a legislator, named a child for him, and confirmed his positive impression shortly before his death. But for all his affection for his master, there was no doubt in his mind that he was a slave. Lively whipped him once. John said he bore him no ill will for it. He said Lively "had to" whip him because he had "cut a fellow with a knife." Determined to make the punishment meaningful, Lively also sent John to jail for a night.[13]

Even assuming there were other unpleasant parts of his

life that memory dimmed, it was an unusual experience for a black slave. During a civil war in which race was the basis for the battles, the teenage slave was permitted, indeed, encouraged, to literacy, given tasks usually reserved for whites in a highly visible institution, and caused no significant hostile comment from the town. He was the heir to Antonio and George, whose reputation and whose patrons still remained in significant positions, albeit in a society about to disappear in defeat. But, evidently, while that society survived, the Proctors still enjoyed some special consideration despite the disability of slavery.

As the war ended, John was twenty-one years old. When it was obvious that Federal troops were about to arrive, county officials loaded all the records in a wagon and sent them to Bainbridge, Georgia, for protection. Some in the town followed the example, among them the Scotts and the Livelys. As John told it some seventy years later, "Mr. Lively sent all his folks to [Albany] Georgia [for ten months] so the Yankees would not get us."[14]

The world had changed by the time John returned, although no one knew how much. Most obvious were the numbers of blue-coated soldiers and the beginning of freedom for black persons. Whites, especially those of prominence and position, appear to have assumed (or at least hoped) that these were the only changes required and that even they might be mitigated in the future. Although they were quickly disabused of that notion, it would be some time before the full impact of defeat and the full magnitude of the change expected of them became obvious.

Despite the hope of Florida government officials, they were not to continue their roles. Union forces reached the capital on May 10, and twelve days later the commander declared martial law. In mid-July President Andrew Johnson appointed William Marvin provisional governor of Florida and instructed him to call a constitutional convention. Marvin, a federal judge from Key West (which had remained in Union hands throughout the war) was a moderate Southerner who arrived in Tallahassee in early August. The new governor was a fit representative of whites in Florida who wished to get on with conducting their affairs as if the war were merely an unpleasant memory.[15] The constitutional convention that met on 25 October shared that outlook. It wrote a document that grudgingly acknowledged the superiority of Northern arms and then reinstated defeated economic, political, and social systems so far as possible. Bowing to the victors, the convention unanimously nullified secession and, by a vote of only twenty to fourteen, abolished slavery. Other actions prohibited blacks from political actions—including voting—and enacted stiff penalties for "vagrancy." The men in Tallahassee came to grief over Florida's Confederate debt. Attempts to weasel on outright repudiation met stern counter-direction from Washington, and the convention meekly accepted repudiation.

Given the suffrage restrictions, unchallenged in Washington, the results of the first election were no surprise. David Walker of Tallahassee was elected governor without opposition. Walker was an old line Whig who had opposed secession but followed his state out of the Union and was elected to the Florida supreme court. The rest of the administration, not surprisingly, had a distinct Whiggish cast. Most of the legislature—and the administration—were former Confederates and until very recently slaveholders.[16]

The actions of the legislature when it met on 18 December surprised no one. It was strongly racist; Governor Walker explained about blacks: "It is not their fault they are free— they had nothing to do with it." All whites (whether Northern or Southern, army or civilian) seemed to agree that society would be best served if blacks remained on the plantations as agricultural laborers. The legislature responded with a black code and white suffrage.[17] Calling the actions of the convention and the legislature reactionary is tempting but hasty. The only truly challenging acts were attempts to fund part of the confederate debt and the election of a member of the house of representatives who could not take the federal test oath. On every other count, people had turned to their traditional moderate leaders, who had responded with what *seemed* moderate measures—including their rejection of the fourteenth amendment the following year.[18]

The United States Congress, now controlled by the Republican party, had a different view of the past—to them Southern moderates were dangerously conservative—and different plans for the future. The Republicans were determined that Southerners understand that the war was not merely a temporary interruption in their lives but that the fundamental order of things had changed. To this end they took control of the Reconstruction process. The South was returned to military rule and new governments required. In addition, Congress made ratification of the fourteenth amendment a condition of readmission and revived and strengthened the Freedmen's Bureau.

The Freedmen's Bureau operated directly on the black population and represented a different level of potential impact. It aimed to provide sustenance and guidance to the freedmen whom white Southerners wished to continue to dominate. As nothing else, it served to make Southerners realize the impact of defeat: it raised the specter of the servile laboring classes vanishing and the appearance of a Republican political force, for it was manned by Republican appointees who saw establishment of their party both as a means to carry out the policy of the victors and, often, as a means of their own advancement. The process would have been easier had there been only two groups in contention for control of the blacks' future—the recent arrivals from the North and the native Southerners. Instead, a new matrix appeared that forever complicated the process of reconstructing Florida (and other Southern States) and, ultimately, doomed hopes of new order.

The Southern whites, now better termed conservatives (Democrats) and moderates (scalawags), initially divided over the related issues of cooperation with the Northern Republican agents of Congress and the nature of treatment of the freedmen. Southern Republicans divided into factions based on their devotion to the national Republican party, the fervency of their commitment to black advancement, and their personal ambition. The moderate Republican faction took control of the party at the 1868 constitutional convention and, although the aims and boundaries of the factions were constantly shifting, generally held control throughout Reconstruction. Led by Northern white and black immigrants (carpetbaggers) and moderate Southern whites (scalawags), the delegates wrote a constitution that, though it gave blacks the vote, permitted the legislature to establish an educational requirement connected to the right. These men wished to build a moderate Republican party by attracting native whites to the banner even at the expense of black advancement and offering strong support to economic development. Thus it was understandable that representation in the legislature favored white counties and gave the governor grand powers of appointment. They also elected the governor, Harrison Reed.[19]

Recruiting blacks and organizing them into the Republican party and its auxiliaries began immediately. For Florida blacks the political invitations represented fulfillment of the promise of the war. Until this point they had been thrown, minus the worst features of slavery, into a labor system on familiar plantations under the control of their former masters—if not individually, at least collectively. Now, at the behest of Congress and often at the mercy of ambitious, recently arrived Northerners, came opportunity.

John Proctor eagerly took advantage of the chance for this new life. At the first opportunity he joined the Republican party; contrary appeals of native white conservatives were unavailing. In his last years John recounted with pride and excitement his participation in a ceremony at the Tallahassee Primitive Baptist Church cemetery, joining one of the secret organizations (probably the Lincoln Brotherhood). In his late twenties, Proctor did more than simply rely on his father's name—assuming that had any value in the new scheme of things—or the power of his patrons to speak for him. From the beginning of his adulthood he established a role independent of Antonio's and George's tradition of working almost exclusively in the local white power structure, almost as if he had read and followed George's exhortations in the *San Francisco*

Elevator. It is important to note that John had a much broader range of options than did his father and his grandfather.

John's first job after freedom was in Wakulla County, immediately to the south of Leon, where he led a crew of men cutting palm trees for shipment to Texas. Soon, however, he appeared as a waiter at the City Hotel. Sometime in the next four years he became a schoolteacher, and he also did farm labor when necessary. He married Mary Mason, who was slightly younger than he. James Smith, the pastor who married them, was the husband of Lydia Smith and had recently also performed the ceremony for John's brother George. John and Mary began a family quickly: John was born in 1869 and Julia in 1870. They would be followed by four others within a decade.[20]

Before 1870, John must have made a conscious decision to go into politics. He, unlike his brothers, stayed in or close to Tallahassee and, like his father and grandfather, did not start the land acquisition process that led to agriculture. He had the advantages that came from being George's and Antonio's heir. He was literate, he had been raised partially by upper class whites, he had experience in town life, and he, obviously, felt at home with both races and moved easily between them. Advancement in his new career came rapidly. At some point he was appointed one of nine commissioners on a task to inspect facilities at Key West and spent six months there; he also worked as a clerk in the Tallahassee Post Office. The postmaster, also black, was William G. Stewart, a full-bearded, one-armed leader of the burgeoning Republican party in Leon County.[21] By 1870 he was recognized in the party and in the county as a full fledged politician—that year he won nomination for the legislature.

John's brothers and sisters chose different paths, paths that make it more difficult to reconstruct the courses of their lives. The other boys rapidly established their independence and their own households. By 1870 Bahamia had married and by the age of twenty-eight was the father of three children: Robert, age eight; Florida, five years old; and the baby George, born that year. He and his wife Juda (or Judy) *both* listed their occupations as "work on farm." At the time he rented in neighboring Jefferson County from Mr. Finlayson, his former owner. George, married to Louisa Williams in January, was nineteen years old in 1870. He, too, called himself a farm laborer; Louisa said her occupation was "keeping house." Their first child was not born until 1878.[22]

Both Bahamia and George became substantial farmers. Although George would serve one term in the Florida House of Representatives and run for election to the 1885 constitutional convention from Jefferson County, his course was clear: no town life and political speculation was in his future. He rejected his older brother's, his father's, and his grandfather's professions in favor of husbandry and by 1900 would own 180 acres free and clear from mortgage. Bahamia's course seemed even more resolute: no stain of political activity ever appeared on his career. He produced a large family and, although he did not acquire land in his own name until much later, quickly became a solid, rural, citizen.

Charlotte, unmarried in 1870, had two children and was still living in the Scott household, employed as a house servant. In 1874 she would marry James Vaughan. She, like her brother John, chose to open an account in the Freedmans Bank where the bank official commented that her paperwork "seems quite intelligent." Nancy, with her husband and daughter, lived nearby. By this time, probably because they had married out of the county, Mary and Georgianna—both still living—had passed from the census taker's view.[23]

The perilous term in the family's life had passed, and all had survived and prospered. The loss of their energetic, committed father did not prevent them from growing into energetic, committed adults. The children's character was the result of their parents' guidance. Even though the youngest barely knew their father, they remained in the family unit for almost a decade after his departure under their mother's tutelage. There was also a genetic factor, and whether it or learned behavior in the family unit was more important is not discernable. The guidance, support, and protection they received from white patricians was also important.

John made clear in his reminiscences the role the three white patricians had played in his upbringing. All the children and Nancy derived the same benefits. Until the late 1850s they were with the Rutgerses, with additional oversight and guidance from Benjamin Allen. The Scotts and Finlaysons were of the same ilk: white, of considerable means, and patrician to the core. Until the challenge of the late 1860s, these men continued their class' dominant role in small isolated Tallahassee, and they continued the stewardship of the Proctors. They were worthy successors to the Simmons, DuVals, Calls, and Walkers.

By 1870 this class suffered a loss of mastery—albeit temporary. For the Proctors the loss was also significant. On one hand it was a liberating force, for it opened the way for them to move forward without the guidance—and restraint—of their patrons. On the other hand, it also removed the safety net this class had provided for them for generations. Because the challenge of Reconstruction also challenged the patricians' philosophy of mutuality of class and race interests in the South—a philosophy that must have been absorbed by these white-raised and white-protected black Proctors—it also drove a real wedge between the Proctors and their patrons. No more would white Floridians be identified with an ambitious Proctor. That position would be reserved for carpetbaggers and temporary political allies. In a sense it was Reconstruction in microcosm. Individuals were given freedom and opportunity without the balancing patrician paternalism. At this most basic level would the victorious North's ideal be tested.

EIGHT

John the Politician

Leon County, throughout Reconstruction, had an absolute majority of black persons. In terms of registered voters, the disparity between the races was even greater. Just after Congress had taken control of the reconstructing process in 1867, the voter lists (skewed by congressional directives) showed a six to one black advantage.[1] Those statistics were at odds with the state as a whole, where whites predominated. But Tallahassee was the capital, and for that reason the black majority there always had special significance. The majority was absolute and symbolic at once. In Reconstruction's early years it exalted the status of elected representatives there; in later years it would doom them to token status in the state and the government. It also facilitated (as it always has) the operations of elected officials since they were in daily contact with all branches of state government and likewise enhanced their effectiveness.

Black citizens were a new phenomenon as, indeed, were black leaders. Both were regarded as a prize by whites, whether native Southern conservative Democrats; immigrant Northern Republicans—moderate or radical (carpetbaggers); or native white moderate Republicans (scalawags). Each saw the numerous, untutored black citizens as the votes necessary to vanquish their opponents. Democrats naively believed their former slaves would follow their former masters; scalawags had the same belief but were willing to offer the former slaves a reward for allegiance; and carpetbaggers trusted that the former slaves' resentment of their former masters was all the motivation needed for their appeal.

John Proctor was not recognized as a leader within the Leon County black community or the black political structure in 1867; at twenty-three years old, he was simply too young and inexperienced. Several men vied for recognition as black leaders. The person who came closest to being recognized as such was Charles H. Pearce, known in Tallahassee as "Bishop" Pearce.[2] Pearce arrived in Tallahassee on 1 March 1866 as the African Methodist Episcopal Church's designated pastor for Florida. A man of great ability and magnetism, he had an immediate impact on both races. His natural organizing ability rapidly built new congregations in the area and gave him great prominence. He understood how to use his power. "A man in this State cannot do his whole duty as a minister," he explained, "except he looks out for the political interests of his people. They are like a ship at sea, and they must have somebody to guide them; and it is natural that they should get their best informed men to lead them." Pearce proceeded to do just that. It was no accident that Pearce was from the organized black Protestant church. Most black leaders at this time were—James Page, James Smith, John Wyatt, John Stokes, and Jonathan Gibbs among them. Once the plantations and slavery were destroyed, the church was the only familiar institution remaining for the former slaves, and it spoke to their aspirations, ultimate and earthly.[3]

The school system grew rapidly and came to prominence in the lives of black persons at this time. Like the church, it offered black people institutional leadership and promised individual betterment. It provided opportunities for employment, promotion, position, and prestige for teachers second only to ministers. It was probably no accident that John Wallace and Proctor were both schoolteachers. Lydia Stout Smith, from the Proctor household of the 1850s, now married to the Reverend James Smith, chose the same course. The redoubtable Charles Dyke, Democratic eminence grise and editor of the *Floridian,* praised her educational work and congratulated her; he also called for "encouragement" for this "well-known colored lady" in her church work. She was, almost certainly, the subject of the Freedmen's Bureau inspector in 1865 who described a school of "interesting girls" in Tallahassee. The teacher, a "mulatto woman of education," announced that she intended "to make ladies of these girls."[4] Lydia was denied further advancement by her sex, and one can only speculate what she might have achieved. Similarly, we have no idea of the nature of any continuing influence she may have had on John Proctor, with whom she maintained a lifelong friendship.[5]

John Wallace was probably the best known schoolteacher, and he eventually eclipsed Bishop Pearce as the premier black leader in Leon County. Wallace was an illiterate North Carolina slave who enlisted in the Union army in 1863. He, too, arrived in Tallahassee in 1866 as a discharged veteran who had taught himself to read and write. He quickly entered Republican politics and, like Proctor, supported himself by teaching school when not on the state payroll. He was marvelously effective as a broker between native whites and Republicans and remained a power in state and local politics into the 1880s. His tortured course revealed the dilemma that would face John Proctor and all black men of character and ambition—whether to trust white preceptors (in either party) or to develop indigenous leadership. Wallace further distinguished himself by leaving a perceptive, but suspect, reminiscence, *Carpet-bag Rule in Florida*, composed with the aid of William Bloxham, the dominant Democrat of Florida politics who was his benefactor and ally.[6]

John's 1870 nomination signaled his approach to the leadership ranks, although as the candidate of the moderate, white-sponsored local Republican faction. For the son of a man who had always worked with white sponsors and patrons, it was probably a very natural and comfortable position. That year two loose factions competed within the party: the Ring, which was moderate and devoted to the national party, headed by Freedmen's Bureau Officer (and soon-to-be-United States Senator) Thomas Osborn; and the radicals, at that time called the Mule Team, headed by Daniel Richards (former treasury agent from Illinois), Liberty Billings (former army officer) and William U. Saunders (a black immigrant from Maryland). In Leon County Bishop Pearce and John Wallace were identified with the Mule Team and Proctor, along with Reverend Page, leaned toward the Ring or, as one student put it, the "white-folks" ticket.[7]

The two factions were divided by three questions that could never be answered and that in time doomed the Florida Republican party: whether the national or the state party took precedence; whether black party leadership was wise and appropriate; and whether the ambition of some of the leaders could be subordinated to the party's needs. The schism was described, somewhat imperfectly, by the conservative *Floridian* when it termed the Pearce ticket "foreign" and characterized the Page-Proctor ticket as being of "native colored men who will no doubt make a good run."[8]

The *Floridian*, of course, had its own point of view—white, native Southern, and conservative. Historically the official paper of the state government and the Democratic party, it now saw state printing given to Republican newspapers and the very existence of its party threatened. Representing the old order, it implored whites to "keep our good old State from being Africanized"—by organizing and registering to vote—and counseled blacks that "no greater misfortune could befall both races than the stirring up of strife and antagonism" since "our interests are one." In March 1869 the paper underwent a change in ownership, and the redoubtable Charles E. Dyke became sole owner and editor.[9]

Dyke, who had first appeared in Tallahassee in 1839, was a major force in Florida politics. His eye remained firmly fixed on the restoration of white, conservative rule; he was by nature patient and understanding; he knew that such an end would take time. He obviously believed that change did not proceed in a straight line, and he participated in initiating much of the misdirection. But he leaned more toward the paternalistic rather than the energetic redeemer, the patrician rather than the fire-eater. He applauded black education and community building; he went to black social events—and spoke at them; and he put the national Liberal Republican ticket at his masthead in 1872.[10] He would have much to do with John Proctor's career.

The 1870 Leon County election was unique in that not only was there no Democratic (conservative) ticket, but that there were no white people on the legislative ballot. The only contest was between the competing Republican factions. The Page-Proctor ticket lost by a two to one margin. Much changed in the next two years. There was, first of all, a partial factional realignment in the county. Despite the obvious enmity between the white Republican administration led by Governor Harrison Reed and the local Pearce-Wallace faction at the polls and in the legislature, the two moved together. A new local ally of the Ring (Osborn) faction, led by John Stokes, a black minister, and E.C. Weeks, a white former Union cavalry officer, appeared in the county.

John Proctor was part of this shift: in his case, however, growth seems a more accurate description of his movement. Briefly put, he left behind his adherence to the familiar Tallahassee leadership (black and white) that he had grown up with and, instead, cast his lot with the carpetbaggers. This alignment lasted for a decade. Proctor and his compatriots—including Pearce and Wallace—were fervent in their devotion to gaining a share of political leadership positions for blacks. Just as important, they remained devoted, almost exclusively, to local rather than national events. Theirs was a grass-roots Republican party in every sense of the word. They aimed to use the political processes to improve the lot of Leon County's population—and that population was overwhelmingly black.

Yet this new alignment was not exclusively a black or exclusively a local affair. The significant figure in it was Simon Conover. Conover, a physician from New Jersey, was a former army officer serving as state treasurer in the Reed administration. He was a hard player at the political game, a Republican who seems to have found the party's platform as comfortable as he did its potential for his personal advancement. Conover's sympathy for black aspirations created a dilemma for him, a dilemma that bound his personal success to the tides of moderate Republicanism. He was, after all, an ambitious carpetbagger in a state where most ambitious white carpetbaggers paid little more than lip service to black advancement. Only so long as radical Republicans held sway in Washington would Conover prosper. He became John Proctor's political mentor.[11]

The election year itself was even more factious than usual. Gubernatorial politics were at work: Reed could not succeed himself, and Thomas Osborn and the Ring wanted to control that nomination as well as the party in general. The competition made the usual factious spring legislative session even more vituperative. Following the session Proctor became very visible, stumping the county for himself, Conover and the others in his faction. By August, nomination time, the two competing Republican organizations within the county had completed their realignment and perfected their organizations.[12] As expected, two Leon County Republican conventions were held that August. The more numerous—the Ring-Stokes-Weeks faction—met in the courthouse; the Conover-Pearce-Wallace-Proctor group gathered in the state senate chamber. Both factions elected slates of delegates to the state convention (Proctor among them) and chose county executive committees.[13]

The already complicated situation was made confusing by national politics in the liberal Republican movement. The Northern liberal Republicans were politicians and reformers who were mightily offended by the scandals of the Grant administration and more interested in national reconciliation than they were in ensuring the permanence of the great social experiment. Those who remained devoted to Reconstruction remained Grant loyalists. Since the Ring was headed by Senator Osborn, who owed his position and patronage control to Grant, the factions in Florida had opposite meanings from the national lexicon.

In other words, John Proctor in 1872 was a local leader of the faction that in national terms opposed the current president, supported a Democrat (Horace Greeley) for that office, leaned toward a softening of the moral strictures of Reconstruction, and looked sympathetically on a return of Southern Democrats to power. Of course he probably disagreed with most of those things, but such was the unreality of Florida politics. Men like Proctor were forced into choices, often by the selfish, immigrant whites who controlled the party's destiny— Conover among them. To the point, had Osborn not been a Grant man, the Conover-Pearce-Wallace faction would have had the option of being on the side of the national Republicans, who continued to support Reconstruction and black advancement.

The Florida State Republican Convention convened in early August. These were high times in the capital city. Early in the morning of 7 August, the *Floridian* commented, "the colored people began to crowd into town from every direction; the old men, the boys, the women and children came in most countless numbers, and by 10 o'clock there must have been between ten and twelve hundred on the streets. As usual on such occasions, the men and boys formed their processions and with drum and fife paraded up and down and down and up." The local factionalism carried over into the convention and, when the Ring-dominated credentials committee offered to compromise by sharing control of the local delegation, the Conover forces seceded. After the convention nominated the native Floridian Ossian Hart for governor, it made a further attempt at conciliation by offering Pearce the position of national elector. Conover strode to the rostrum and explained that Pearce was "sick in bed" and declined the honor for him.[14]

Following adjournment the drama continued. A liberal Republican delegation (including Proctor) was elected from Leon County and sent to the state liberal Republican convention in Jacksonville. That convention met at the same time as the state Democratic (termed "conservative") convention and voted to endorse the Democratic candidates. The delegates from Leon County bolted at this point. Whether they left because they were unable to stomach the event or because, as the *Floridian* accused, they could not get Conover nominated for any state office is not clear. They returned home and chose their own ticket for local offices: Bishop Pearce for senate, and for the assembly, John Wyatt, John Wallace, William Stewart, and John E. Proctor.[15]

The electoral stakes were made higher by the knowledge that the legislature would choose a United States senator. The Osborn-Ring faction had won the gubernatorial nomination, and their opponents believed it imperative that they not be given the senatorship as well. Their plans to capture the seat, obviously agreed upon in advance by Governor Reed, the Florida Democrats, and Treasurer Conover, were revealed in a meeting at Conover's capitol office. The proposition was simple: in exchange for a dollar figure equaling the pay to be earned by a member of the Florida assembly, Wallace was asked to withdraw from the ticket so that Conover could have a seat in the legislature, which would give him a leg up in the senatorial election. Wallace refused. The same proposition was put to John Wyatt. He accepted but only if the money were paid up front rather than after the election results.[16] With that modification, the entire ticket was elected, and John Proctor became a member of the Florida lower house.[17]

Reviewing the events of the campaign—and knowing that Reconstruction would fail—it is very easy to see Proctor (and Wallace, Pearce, Stewart, and Wyatt) as instruments of the immigrant whites, the carpetbaggers. They were not. They were intelligent, determined men seeking opportunity to gain control of their own—and their race's—destiny. That issue was, after all, one of the major reasons for the continued factionalism in the party. They worked hard at organizing their own and were quickly on the verge of controlling Leon County politics.[18] They saw their alliance with white Republicans as a door opening. It did, and in Leon County the blacks were able to walk through. That opening, however, did not exist in the rest of the state.

When the legislature met in Tallahassee on 7 January 1873, neither Republican faction conceded the advantage. Each, obviously, wished to control the organization of the assembly and, thus, have an advantage in electing a senator who would control the federal patronage. The great danger lay in the narrowness of the Republican majority: there were twenty-five Democrats in the assembly and only twenty-eight Republicans. Only twenty-two appeared at the Republican caucus. One member had not yet arrived and another five—Proctor and Wallace among them—boycotted. The Ring-dominated gathering chose a black member, John R. Scott of DuVal, as the Republican candidate for speaker. It was not a choice made because white Republicans were dedicated to the advancement of blacks or from the power of black Republicans themselves. The Ring, rather, chose Scott because he was thought to be pliable and because, it was believed, no anti-Ring Republican could vote against a black.

But the Ring was out-maneuvered; Conover's team had planned better and their alliance held. On opening day, despite pressure and intimations of violence, Assemblyman Wallace nominated Simon Conover for speaker, and, with Democratic support, he was elected.[19] The bargain was explicit: Democrats would have a share in running the assembly, and federal patronage would not be limited to white Republicans—Democrats and blacks would have a share. Implicit in the deal was a Democratic willingness to be supportive of a moderate course in state government. Everyone except the Ring politicians saw great advantage. Conover got to be speaker—and senator—and the faction he represented won the opportunity to build a permanent majority of former Whigs, converted Democrats, recent immigrants, and blacks in Florida. Democrats achieved immediate entry to the spoils and power. And the blacks—the Bishop Pearces, the John Wallaces, and the John Proctors—took a big step, they thought, up the political ladder.

John Proctor did very well in the bargain. He was appointed to the committee on finance and taxation and the committee on privileges and election; he was chairman of the committee on public printing. His role clearly identified him (at age twenty-nine) as part of the leadership: he offered motions on the floor, his bills passed, he was one of the members who kept the flow of business moving during the session.[20]

Speaker Conover moved quickly to consummate the Democratic bargain. He appointed H.L. Mitchell, a Democrat, as chairman of the judiciary committee and packed the committee on privileges and elections to enforce the partnership. The committee consisted of three trustworthy Republicans, including Proctor, and two Democrats; John Wallace was chairman. In previous sessions this committee had controlled membership of the House through its rulings on disputed elections. It did so again in 1873, except that now some Democrats were declared winners, and the Ring members uniformly lost.[21]

Control of the membership was the key to the senatorial election. Even with Conover as speaker, his election was no sure thing. Before the vote, each disputed seat was fought not so much for the righteousness of the process as for the potential federal spoils. Pressure on the committee to unseat Democrats in favor of Ring adherents was intense. Bribery was a common avenue of exploration. In one case an Osborn manager approached Proctor and offered him seven hundred dollars to swing the committee in favor of a Ring candidate. Proctor took the money, bought two mules for his farm, reported the incident to Wallace and voted against the Ring candidate. A second attempt centered on trying to corrupt Representative Stewart of Leon County. He threw the money on the ground in disgust, "whereupon the briber told him he was a crazy man, picked up the envelope and put it in his pocket." Assemblyman Proctor, learning of the incident, allowed as how he "would take all the money he had to give away." Proctor, obviously, was not offered another chance.[22]

Challenges out of the way, legislators moved to the senatorial election. The Ring politicians, now led by Marcellus Stearns (former army officer and Freedmen's Bureau official) met at the City Hotel and decided that they would support the Democrat James D. Westcott, Jr., son of former senator Westcott, who had been George Proctor's attorney. A Democrat who learned of the bargain told Charles Dyke, who had a previous bargain with Conover. Dyke chose to uphold the previous bargain and in combination with the Wallace-Pearce-Proctor forces determined the outcome.

Balloting in joint session began on 21 January and proceeded for ten days, taking twenty ballots in all. On the first fifteen attempts Proctor voted for Conover whose strength wavered from thirty-two on ballot eleven to six on ballot fifteen. On the next three votes Proctor left Conover whose totals were four, four and twenty. On ballot nineteen, Proctor returned to Conover whose vote was twenty-six. On ballot twenty, Conover won with forty-three—Proctor's and eighteen other black members votes included. The outcome, said Charles Dyke, was "reason to rejoice." Conover, the prime Democrat concluded, "sympathized with our sufferings" and opposed "those greedy cormorants and insatiable vampyres who, as a band of carpet-bag adventurers after the war, fastened themselves upon the subject communities of the South only to suck our remaining substance and batten upon our misery." [23]

The major legislation to come out of the session was a civil rights bill. It was a significant step for black persons, providing equal access to essentially all public institutions supported by taxation, prohibiting discrimination on juries, and prohibiting the use of the word "white" to encourage lack of access. Taking no chances, the bill was not referred to the judiciary committee with its Democrat chairman but instead to a select committee who obviously gave a favorable report. On 17 January, midway in the senatorial election marathon, it passed the house thirty to twenty, Proctor in the majority. (Three Democratic votes were necessary to secure passage in the senate.) When signed into law, it did not provide means to prohibit segregation in private institutions, including private schools. It was, nonetheless, a real step forward. [24]

Most of the remainder of business concerned the factional sniping, which had, and would, characterize the Republican party. Ring members of the legislature made half-hearted attempts to overturn Conover's election to the senate. In response, Proctor, speaking for the Conover forces, questioned Governor Hart's appointments to state offices. No one expected that to produce results, but the Pearce-Wallace-Proctor-led blacks were successful in forcing Governor Hart to appoint Jonathan Gibbs, a black, to his cabinet. To rub a little salt in the Ring's wounds—and to keep good their bargain with the Democrats—Proctor, as chairman of the committee on public printing, led the legislature in keeping the Ring candidate from achieving the post of state printer and threw it instead to Hamilton Jay. Jay had been Conover's chief clerk and was now a partner, albeit temporarily, of Charles Dyke in the printing business.[25] By the time of adjournment, Proctor and all his faction had reason for satisfaction. In six short months he had risen from his schoolteacher/laborer background to a position of consequence in state politics. He was not a controller of events (few blacks in Florida ever reached that position), but he was a factor in events and would long be one.

The party, or more properly, the Conover faction of the party, had done well too. Although they had lost the governorship, they had controlled the assembly, elected the patronage-dispensing senatorship, and broken the power of the Ring in the capital. Such advances seemed to auger well for Proctor and his party, but in Florida's Reconstruction politics there were never any good bets.

At first all seemed to go well. The Conover Republicans and the Dyke Democrats met, congratulated themselves on their work, and, while neither was willing to give up their heritage or their hopes, agreed to continue their joint work in opposing the Ring. The bargain seemed to hold: Conover achieved federal appointments for not only whites of his faction but for blacks and some Democrats. The Democrats followed a middle course publicly. The *Floridian*, for example, upheld the rights of a whites-only policy at the local skating rink but counseled that a "rink for the exclusive enjoyment of colored people" was likewise necessary. When it came to the black Fourth of July celebration, the paper described a celebration where the speakers said nothing but what "every one could heartily respond to." (Senator Conover lead the speakers, Proctor was prominently featured.)[26]

That September, the self-serving editor Dyke gave John Proctor center stage in the continuing Republican controversy. In recognition of his position in the party, the *Sentinel* (whose editor Proctor had kept from becoming state printer) castigated Proctor for his disloyalty to the Hart administration and the Republican party in general. Subsequent issues attacked Senator Conover as well and accused Proctor of threatening the editors with "the terrors of the so-called Ku-Klux or some other *personal violence.*" Proctor replied through space given him in the *Floridian.* Disavowing any knowledge of the Klan (which was hard at work in neighboring counties), he indignantly defended his right to oppose those who worked for "purely selfish and unworthy ends" and called Conover the best hope in "bringing about an era of good feeling among the people."[27] For Proctor, the exchange boded well—it confirmed his position of significance. But for the Democrats it played better: supporting the Proctors of the world aided in destroying the unity of the Republican party. Nowhere, unfortunately, does any record of the black Republicans' reaction, or understanding, of such events exist.

When the legislature met again on 6 January 1874, Simon Conover had removed to Washington, and the agony of electing a new speaker again challenged the assemblymen. As in the previous year, it was not a simple thing, for without their leader, the Conover faction was at a disadvantage. Whatever the cause, and John Wallace later attributed it to the Ring "stratagem," enough Democrats supported the carpetbagger state prison warden and member of the assembly, Malachi Martin, to elect him speaker. Martin clearly was not a strong Ring politician, but he leaned closely enough toward that faction to earn negative votes from Proctor and his colleagues. Speaker Martin showed he understood: Proctor did not get a committee chairmanship, although he was appointed to the committee on claims and the committee on incorporations— both committees of significance.[28]

Bad blood between the speaker and the Proctor forces continued throughout the session. It reached a peak when an assembly committee charged with inspecting the state prison came to grief at the orders of the warden/speaker. A special train that was to carry them to the prison, "fortified" with wines, whiskeys, and cigars, John Wallace later asserted, left two hours early at Martin's orders so that the two black members would miss the train. The missing assemblymen made their way to the prison on their own but were forcibly ejected from the visiting party during the tour on orders from Martin himself. In the days following the debacle Proctor responded by introducing measures creating a select committee to investigate the matter. That measure passed, and, when the members waffled on assigning blame for the contretemps, Proctor joined others who were trying, unsuccessfully, to censure Martin. Calmer heads, however, carried the day, and the whole matter died without further issue.[29]

Despite their factional contest, the Republicans ruled the legislature. Once the speakership was out of the way, little else of consequence existed to prolong the intraparty contest: the quieting of the prison investigation fiasco in point. Even Proctor, point man of the anti-Ring, anti-administration, anti-speaker forces, did well. Martin appointed him to important standing committees and to a select committee, and he played a significant role in conducting the daily course of business in the Assembly. Of the five bills he introduced, three passed. For a person who, clearly, was no longer a member of the leadership's inner circle, he remained a power in the lower chamber. Part of that power, obviously, came from his close identification with Senator Conover, but part of it came from his growing stature in Leon County and Florida political circles.[30]

The main business of the session revolved around Florida's attitude toward business. "Southern law," Eric Foner has explained, was rapidly being "redesigned so as to encourage the free flow of capital and enhance the property rights of corporations," a concept supported by black legislators who sought to "enrich their communities." The Florida legislature now designed a general incorporation act for railroads and canals that among other things, eliminated the necessity of individual legislative authorization for each corporation. Proctor, a member of the committee on incorporations, signed the committee report recommending passage of the bill but, for unknown reasons, voted against it on final passage. Most Republicans voted for it. Amendments to the state constitution prohibiting the use of the state's credit to aid individuals or corporations and requiring taxation of all corporate property (except that used for religious, educational, or charitable purposes) also took much time during the session. On these, the Republicans acted like a modern, unified party. Although there were individual voting variations on some minor procedural and detail matters, on all significant votes, the Republicans, including John Proctor, voted for achievement of their party platform.[31]

Republicans reached their zenith during this two year period in office. They controlled the executive and legislative branches of the government and managed to translate much of their party platform into state policy. In terms of the aims of Reconstruction, for the first time black politicians were a significant factor in the business of the state. They were numerous and, with men like Proctor, Wallace, and Pearce among them, too ambitious and intelligent to be ignored. From the appearance of government, the revolution in Southern life and Southern politics appeared to be becoming institutionalized.

But appearances were not utterly reflective of the situation. In Leon County the factional contest never stopped. John Proctor, chairman of the Republican county executive committee, issued a call early in July for the county nominating convention only to find that there was still in existence the other Republican county executive committee headed by E.C. Weeks. Weeks, who had been appointed county sheriff by the Hart administration, called an opposing convention for the same day.

It was enough to gladden the heart of any Democrat— although the party was still so weak in Leon County it could not nominate a ticket itself. The Republicans, too, knew the disaster that loomed with a split party, so efforts proceeded from both factions to bring the fighters together. They failed, partially, it seems clear, because of the efforts of the state administration, which did not want to share anything with the Proctor-Wallace black Leon County faction.[32]

Efforts at reconciliation failing, both factions nominated

full tickets for the legislature. The contest was bitter. John Wallace carried the banner for Leon County's senate seat, and John Proctor was the acknowledged head of the assembly ticket—all black. They campaigned hard, for the division between factions in the county was deep, and the balance was close. Even though Proctor and Wallace were sitting members and highly popular among the rank and file, Tallahassee was the capital with a sitting governor who opposed the two and who appointed local officials—including Sheriff Weeks—who shared his view.

The bitterness of the campaign paled beside the vote-counting process. It seems clear that the Stearns-Weeks faction, controlling county electoral machinery, attempted an out-and-out steal of the election. Charges of intimidation, illegal voting, and technical errors were common; the most flagrant violation came in Centerville—power base of the Stearns-Weeks faction. There the votes for the Wallace-Proctor ticket were simply lost. The clerk later testified that the vote for Proctor and others was counted "on a piece of paper which was not attached to the papers containing a list of the other votes cast at said precinct for want of mucilage with which to so attach it." Had the disputed precincts been discounted, the Wallace-Proctor slate would have been defeated. The local courts, however, were still in the hands of their adherents, and, when they judged the returns, the disputed votes all went to the incumbents, giving them an almost two hundred vote majority (out of 2,700 votes cast.)[33]

John Proctor led the Leon County assembly ticket—testament to his political star's rise—and when the legislature met on 5 January 1875, his star continued ascending. He was, after all, Senator Conover's leading black lieutenant, he had done well in his position the previous session, and he had just been reelected at the head of his ticket.

The Conover-Dyke alliance controlled the organization of the legislature and all its work. Cooperation was vital in the evenly divided session. (The parties were evenly split in the senate; there were three more Democrats than Republicans in the assembly, but a few independent members represented potential control.) This time the bargain was for a moderate Democrat as speaker, black Republicans as subordinate officers (chief clerk, sergeant, and others), and appropriate committee assignments for anti-Ring Republicans. For the initial ballots, William W. Hicks of Dade County was the choice of the coalition, and when he could not win a majority, Proctor led a group of black legislators to vote for Thomas Hannah of Washington County who won on the sixth ballot. Proctor was recognized for his timely choice by appointment as one of a committee of three to escort the new speaker to the chair. Real reward came with his appointment as chairman of the committee on legislative expenses and as a member of the committee on public printing—neither committee important for the substantial legislation it might consider, but both important for political control.[34]

Assemblyman Proctor was a member of consequence. His two bills of substance—one to repeal the General Incorporation Act for Canals and Railroads and one to permit county officers to practice law while holding office—did not pass, but other substantive resolutions and motions did. He voted with the majority to make Charles Dyke the state printer—a litmus test of the coalition. On balance, he supported the coalition as would have been expected. Of eighty-two record votes that were not unanimous votes and on which Proctor and Hannah voted, Proctor voted with the speaker forty-seven times and against him thirty-five times.[35]

The clearest indications of Proctor's position and power came in two separate incidents. The first concerned the failed Freedmans Savings Bank. Aside from the signal its failure gave about the progress of Reconstruction and aside from the hardship its failure brought to poor black depositors, the failure furnished occasion for debate and name-calling on the assembly floor. Embarrassing as it was for this Reconstruction institution to fail, the coalition Republicans in the assembly could not permit their Ring opponents to agitate the issue. So, when a Ring assemblyman offered legislation concluding that the failure was "inspired by a hatred of the Union and the colored race, and intended to injure the Republican party,"

John Proctor quickly led the coalition to remove the offensive language.[36]

The second occasion was the election of a United States senator for Florida's second seat. This was one of those issues on which the members of the coalition had agreed to disagree. In the prolonged contest (twenty-four ballots in all) no candidate of ability and integrity survived. In the end the legislature turned to a foreign-born former carpenter from Pensacola, distinguished only for his mediocrity. No black could vote for the winner, Charles W. Jones, but in a complement to John Proctor's position, his block of thirteen cast all their votes for him on the third ballot.[37]

For John Proctor, son of George and grandson of Antonio, Reconstruction meant salvation. He was a member of the government his grandfather had worked for; he sat in the legislature his father had watched. He was lauded by the leading Democrat in Florida, and he spoke as the chief black lieutenant of the United States senator. The choices he had made had borne results. He now spoke as a full member of the society to which his father and grandfather had sought, and been denied, admittance. Like his forebears, he worked with white persons who were critical of his advancement. But, breaking new ground for the Proctor men, John's relationships were not the traditional patrician ones but rather were more modern business/political relationships. Unfortunately, the South was not ready to institutionalize its new, unwanted system. By the time rejection of that system was complete, John Proctor's new ground had been swept from beneath him.

NINE

The End of Reconstruction

John Proctor did not know Reconstruction was about to end any more than his father had realized that the panic of 1837 was about to engulf him. Neither comprehended, nor did many—perhaps most—other Americans, that the guideposts and assumptions of the current order of things were about to be challenged and overwhelmed. In the case of Reconstruction, passage of time had weakened the ardor of its congressional leaders. As the giants of the war generation passed from the scene, their successors, who paid lip service to the war's ideals, had more interest in national reconciliation, less faith in black ability, and a more conservative view of society and government than their predecessors. This gave these Northern pillars of government and society much in common with the white Democrats of the South. As that commonality grew, so did the challenge to Reconstruction.[1]

This was not apparent, in early 1876, to Assemblyman Proctor. The former waiter cum schoolteacher and Republican legislator had a new job: he had become chief clerk in the United States surveyor general's office located in Tallahassee. There would be no legislative session in 1876, and Proctor, who had left schoolteaching behind and who never was a successful—or interested—farmer, obviously needed a respectable and financially secure position. Another Conover lieutenant, this one white, had been appointed surveyor general in May. LeRoy D. Ball had been in Tallahassee some years and fully supported the coalition-building of Senator Conover and editor Dyke. He was very active in Republican politics, but the kind of Republican politics that led the *Floridian* to gush about his "superior intelligence . . . pleasant manners . . . [and] moderate views." Of Ball's new deputy, Mr. Dyke waxed ecstatic. Proctor, he noted, was native born (not a carpetbagger), earned an honest living, and "enjoys in a high degree the confidence of his race, and is also much respected by the white people." Dyke wished that "all the colored people of the county were like John E. Proctor." [2]

The new chief clerk had increased financial obligations. His family had grown, and he needed to provide for their future. Four children lived at home in 1876: John, the first born who was seven; Julia, six, who would start school that year; Henrietta, born in 1873; and Mary, the baby, born in 1875. The thirty-six-year-old father had never owned real property. Instead he rented his house, and the tax collector concluded that his total taxable property was worth a modest $265. The livestock he kept (one to four cows and up to six hogs) suggested he was doing no more farming than was necessary to supply his family's immediate needs. Interestingly, Proctor owned three horses in 1875-1876 whereas he owned only one mule in 1874, which gives some support to the bribery story if he purchased horses instead of mules. [3] It would be two years before Proctor could afford to buy land of his own.

But in 1876, John must have thought the future was his for the asking. It was not simply a matter of his personal advancement since 1870—he was an important member of the ruling coalition. He was not an originator or a controller; that role was reserved to Conover and Dyke, the most visible and powerful of many influential people who participated. Charles Dyke, speaking for native Southerners who were not Republican, had learned his lesson in the late 1860s. He and his party knew that as long as Northerners supported Republican Reconstruction, Southern Democrats would not regain control of the government, especially within Leon County. Yet they remained a potent force in their own right. In the 1874 election they won twenty-five of fifty-three seats in the assembly, and control of the senate was evenly divided. Much of their potency was based on their opponent's weaknesses; the Republicans were never able to build a unified party. The issues that divided them six years earlier continued to keep the party badly split. Neither half would concede the advantage, and neither could rule by themselves.

It is not known which partner in the coalition had made the first move. It mattered little, for working together was the only way to insure a share of power for each. At the beginning of 1876 the coalition continued to work well: the Republican partners had one United States senator and controlled federal patronage; Democrats had the other United States senator, and the speaker of the assembly.[4] Both seats in the house of representatives were held by the Republicans. Each group spoke well of the other. In the Tallahassee municipal elections they had jointly nominated a "Citizens" ticket headed by a white Democrat, and Senator Conover introduced the candidate to a public meeting, saying that "he had long hoped for the time to come when all the people, without distinction of race or party, would meet together and select for office the best men. He was thankful that that time had now come." After the organization of the 1875 assembly, editor Dyke publicly praised the combination "between the Conservatives and Liberals . . . [which] discongrided [sic] . . . the uncompromising, unyielding straight-jacket Ring." Senator Conover helped moderate Democrats to office, and when necessary editor Dyke went to Washington to confer with him. Mrs. Conover socialized with Democratic wives, and Senator Conover would become an honorary member of a Democratic governor's guards—so would LeRoy Ball.[5]

Although all members of the coalition repeated the rhetoric about the potential of a new society based on peace and equality and may have believed it, it is more likely that they viewed the coalition as a temporary expedient. The Conover Republicans joined until they could achieve the upper hand in the state party—undoubtedly through the exercise of national power—and compel their dissident brothers to join them in a permanent Florida electoral majority. The Democrats joined until the Republican split was made permanent, and they could exploit the opening for permanent control. John Proctor was a full player in this game of political opportunism: he won at the polls, and he played at political spoils. He showed himself the true offspring of his father and grandfather. Antonio and George, denied the political opportunity, had aggressively sought advancement in the course of their own lives—Antonio in the military and George in business. They had always known the risks, and George, perhaps underestimating them, had fallen victim to them. Now John had the same judgment to make: he had to determine how much to believe in the dream and how much to prepare for its failure. As with his father and grandfather, there is no way to know how he viewed that question.

The coalition partners, however, came to a divergence in 1876, an election year and a presidential year. Democrats shunned their temporary allies, and Conover Republicans found the Ring much more attractive than they could have ever previously imagined: they, for example, suggested that a black Ring politician, John Stokes, be appointed sheriff of Leon County. Governor Stearns quickly obliged them.[6] This initial show of good faith had important results.

In February Sheriff Stokes, also chairman of the Ring Republican executive committee, contacted John Proctor, chairman of the Conover Republican executive committee, and suggested that a joint meeting of the two committees was appropriate to explore a truce. The initial venture seemed to go well, and a second meeting, this time involving the rank and file, was called for Centerville on 19 February. When that meeting was called to order, attendance was slim, and the sides were so evenly balanced that the two temporary chairmen, Proctor and Stokes, were unable to proceed. After considerable discussion, it was agreed that Postmaster William Stewart (a Proctor benefactor and Conover loyalist) should preside. Then the two ten-man committees consolidated and made a place for the twenty-first member, Stewart. The Ring managers, who had warmly supported the idea of union, were incensed. Their anger increased the following day when in

Tallahassee the consolidated executive committee elected the white LeRoy Ball—another Conover loyalist—as permanent chairman. John Proctor had given up his post as chairman, but he remained on the executive committee and was on the winning side.[7]

The carefully constructed unity was illusory; by April it was gone. The union executive committee exploded, and the two old committees reconstituted, each nominating candidates to the state convention. Proctor, along with Stewart, Wallace, and Conover were among those from the Conover faction. But at the state convention Governor Stearns held the upper hand. Conover's delegation was not admitted—their Leon County opponents were—and after four days of bitter wrangling, the delegates nominated Marcellus Stearns for governor and chose an all-white delegation to the Republican national convention.

Senator Conover immediately led his defeated delegation (including Proctor) and delegates from twenty-five other counties into a rump convention. That meeting, seeking to draw lines between themselves and the Stearns crowd, elected the black, former Florida congressman Josiah Walls their president, nominated Conover for governor, and sent a delegation of equal numbers of blacks and whites to the national convention.[8] It was all downhill from that point. The Republican national convention would not seat the all-white Stearns delegation and welcomed Conover instead—and sent him back to Florida with official recognition of his gubernatorial nomination. But, after appeals, a subsequent meeting of the national committee withdrew that approval and gave the nomination back to Stearns.[9]

Then followed the Leon County Convention to nominate candidates for local and state office. In a carefully controlled move to again restore unity, the current assemblymen were replaced by a divided ticket, including E.C. Weeks. Proctor, loyal politician not renominated for the legislature, accepted delegate status to the congressional nominating convention and remained on the county executive committee. At the congressional nominating convention the unity mode continued until the vote to endorse the Stearns nomination. If the delegates really wanted unity, there they should have engineered it. But one-third (including Proctor, Wallace, and Stewart) voted against Stearns, removing any appearance of accommodation. From that point on, unlike most of his comrades, Proctor appears to have sat out the rest of the contest. Perhaps he could not stomach what followed.[10] The campaign rapidly degenerated. Conover would not withdraw and, obviously with Democratic urging, issued a circular (printed by the *Floridian*) announcing his intent to fight to the finish. Stearns responded by privately offering Conover, Wallace later reported, "twelve to fifteen hundred dollars" to withdraw and bring his friends to support the Ring nominations. Conover took the money, withdrew, and said nothing to his friends.[11]

It is hard to know whom to blame for the fiasco. Distance and lack of primary documentation prevent complete appraisal. If Conover could not swallow the offending resolution at the county convention, Stearns should have withdrawn it. The Stearns faction should have accommodated some black candidates. The Democrats were pleased with the result and happy to fund Conover's destructive candidacy. Even if the major fault lay with Conover, the stakes were high, and there was plenty of blame to spread around.

John Proctor's role was limited to serving as an election supervisor in Leon County.[12] He watched the white Democrats win control of the Florida's executive branch and elect majorities in both houses of the legislature just as he had seen white Republicans bulldoze their way into control of his party. Reconstruction was ending, and John Proctor was returning to private life.

As a private citizen, John found himself at a crossroads. Evidently secure in his clerkship, he had bowed to the requirements of party loyalty only to see his party turn its back on his color and his white coalition partners claim the electoral prizes. But he did not retire from the fight. Whether because of his belief in eventual victory of the Conover faction and the triumph of the coalition or because of some personal inheritance from his father and grandfather, he evidently waited and prepared for the next election.

The coalition was dead: Florida Democrats no longer had a need for it. And, while Governor Drew and the Democratic legislature ended Reconstruction at the state level by enacting their platform into law and replacing the state's Republican officeholders with Democrats, President Hayes in the White House withdrew uniformed United States Army troops from Tallahassee bringing national Reconstruction to an end. He naively believed Southerners were accepting the racial progress and wished, under those circumstances, to return the South to home rule. He appears to have believed, given those conditions, that the Southern Republican party would survive as a credible institution.[13]

Florida blacks, especially those in Leon County, were without position or power; the white wing of the Republican party was in control there. Governor Stearns spent some time after the election trying to force a judicial decision in his favor that would overturn the election. Ironically, Senator Conover was a Hayes supporter and would lead these out-of-government blacks in the direction of the Hayes camp. To clarify the Florida situation, black leaders in Jacksonville sent out a call for a "Colored Convention" on the fourth of July. Proctor, Stewart, and Wallace all came as Leon County delegates. Hayes's managers could not have scripted it better—nor could Florida Democrats.

The principal speaker was their former—and undoubtedly current—champion, Senator Conover. "The immediate political outlook," he concluded, "may not be as inviting as ardent Republicans would desire, but the future" was not necessarily discouraging. The national government was with them, he continued, and the "President's 'Southern policy'" was simply returning their state to self government. Rather than letting themselves be led by unnamed "unscrupulous men," Florida blacks should bow to the "welfare of the community." They should give more attention to economic and individual self-help, to agriculture and industrial pursuits, to education and the elevation of their comrades, and to the perpetuation of the equal rights and equal justice planks of their party. That, rather than political infighting, would bring them happiness and success. The platform called for liberty and equal rights through education, land ownership, and control of intoxicating drink. It hoped that the race issue would pass away. Instead "peace, order, confidence, *more tolerance of opinion than ever before, and better protection to life, liberty and property*" were the keys to prosperity. No one seems to have cared much about electoral reform or using the power of government for desired ends.[14] The platform was a real retreat from the heady achievements of the late 1860s and the early 1870s. Gone were the days when equal rights speeches elicited support; now blacks were urged to quiescence rather than encouraged to action. If John Proctor and other Florida blacks bought the message, the purchase cheapened the quality of their lives considerably. It seems that they did. Perhaps they saw it as a new way to success, an alternate route to sufficiency in their society. In the long run it was more than a momentary setback, an electoral defeat to be avenged with the backing of the national government at the next contest. The national government was saying, after all, that such support was a thing of the past. Perhaps the Proctors, the Wallaces—and the Conovers saw the hope of their future in turning their coalition into a political party, a twist on the Hayes scenario but one that at least had some experiential basis. Or perhaps the seemingly overpowering strength of the Democrats and the campaign of terror against blacks (never a significant thing in Leon County) drove them from their earlier advanced position. That would be at least understandable. But in any case, there was no revolt, only continued obeisance to Conover and his lieutenants.

The election year of 1878 began with the white Democrats and white Republicans firmly in control—and Senator Conover seeing the end of his term fast approaching. Leon County black Republicans scrambled for position. John Wallace, who had just been removed as a justice of the peace by Governor Drew, accused the Democrats of double-dealing by campaigning for black votes and not providing the reward of offices to black supporters. Florida blacks, he threatened, should consider finding new white allies. He promptly began a flirtation with the Greenback party.[15] Proctor did not follow. Whether out of loyalty to or belief in Conover (whose plans he undoubtedly knew), simple inertia, or for some unknown reason, he resisted changing course and continued in the orbit of the coalition. He, unlike Wallace, was promptly rewarded with a new job. In late March he became the agent for the Jacksonville, Pensacola and Mobile Railroad. Controlled by the state administration, the corporation was a wreckage of the grand organ of railroad speculation it had been during Republican Reconstruction. Clearly a reward for loyalty, Proctor's appointment was prominently announced in the *Floridian*.[16]

Proctor's mentor, Simon Conover, sought a seat in the United States House of Representatives; he knew the Democratic legislature—coalition or not—would not reelect him to the United States Senate. But it was not clear that he could control the Leon County delegation to the nominating convention. In fact, he could not. Three months of squabbling ensued, with inevitable meetings, reconciliations, and splits, before the Leon County delegation—headed by Conover rival E.C. Weeks—finally settled itself. John Proctor appears to have worked quietly, but effectively, behind the scenes.[17]

At the district convention, no easy solution to the vexing Republican problem presented itself. The great majority of the delegates were black, and they were unwilling to see the prize go to E.C. Weeks from the white wing of the party. Likewise the black state senator from Jefferson County, Robert Meacham, could not muster a majority. The delegates quickly turned to Senator Conover and endorsed the national administration's policies.

When the Leon County delegates returned home, they had to contend not only with the usual bitterness between their two wings but an announcement from Weeks that he would run as an independent. As predicted, there were two tickets for the legislature. John Proctor, his loyalty and work rewarded, took a place on the assembly ticket, and the wandering John

Wallace returned to the fold and took the senate nomination. Conover carried Leon County but lost in the district at large, and the Wallace-Proctor ticket won election to the legislature, although Wallace's victory came through a protest after he seemingly failed to win by nine votes.[18]

When Assemblyman Proctor returned to his seat in the legislature on 7 January 1879, he found Democrats held forty-six seats and Republicans only twenty-eight. (There was one independent.) Democrats controlled the senate twenty-three to seven. There was no longer any need for the Democrats to participate in coalition politics. The majority party had everything its own way in the legislature. They controlled the organization of the assembly, and, once they had decided on their candidate, Wilkinson Call, they easily elected him to Senator Conover's United States Senate seat.[19]

The 1879 session shows John Proctor to his best advantage. Black legislators during Reconstruction remain an object of wonderment to later generations. Were they simply followers of carpetbaggers? Were they real human beings who were not yet experienced enough for the challenge of governing? Or were they idealists who failed because the federal government left them stranded?

Proctor had no strong party or person to direct him in 1879; neither had he any coalition on which to rely. Even though Leon County Democrats could not prevent Republicans from being elected to the legislature, their statewide majority removed any necessity of pandering at home. Proctor realized as much: he voted against Charles Dyke for state printer during the session.[20] Nor was there any national connection. Washington was a long way off and after 1876 not really paying attention anyway. Proctor, and others like him, were on their own. During the session itself Proctor's behavior confirmed his new found position: on recorded votes that were not unanimous, he was in the minority 125 times and the majority only 89 times.

The Democratic general assembly leadership had no need to heed a thirty-five-year-old without a United States senator or Charles Dyke to back him up. Yet it did. His only standing committee appointment, Corporations, was a substantive one. And Republican Proctor functioned as a full, respected member of the lower house. He was recognized by the speaker as one who helped move along the daily flow of business, he was appointed to two select committees, and his bills and resolutions passed often enough to give him real weight.[21]

The select committee appointments give evidence of the regard in which the controlling Democrats held John Proctor. One was a revenue measure (Assembly bill 167), and the other was a measure of his own. On 17 January he introduced a resolution calling for a joint committee (select) to examine the matter of "Comptroller's Warrants known as Greenback Scrip outstanding" and recommended that the committee be given authority to recall and cancel it. The speaker had full power not to take the resolution, but he did, and it passed. The speaker had no real need to appoint Proctor to the committee, but he did.[22]

Outside the legislature, party affairs beckoned. Republicans still controlled the national government and retained pockets of strength in Florida; they would elect a congressman as late as 1884. Private citizen Conover believed a new coalition could make them a majority and take him to the governor's office. Ninety percent of all Florida Republicans, he believed, endorsed him—it was only the small minority of office-seeking carpetbaggers who refused him support. Many Republicans felt he could appeal to enough former Whigs and dissatisfied Democrats to fashion a majority. He also counted on having the next president to back him. He believed John Sherman, secretary of the treasury, would be that man.[23]

Although national and state politics kept him from being appointed collector of internal revenue at Jacksonville, Conover, at Sherman's hand, was appointed inspector of customs with authority throughout the state, headquartered in Tallahassee. That was very important. Not only did Conover now have significant impact on federal patronage in the state, his champion was a major figure in national politics. "In a period when the major political problems were also financial in their bearing," explains one student of the period, "the Treasury was inevitably the most important among its sister agencies."[24]

Ten months later John Proctor entered the treasury department service as deputy collector at St. Marks. Apparently a vacancy was created for him. Clearly the position was within the power of Conover: whether he wished to reward a loyal disciple and respected Republican, to create a vacancy in the Leon County delegation to help build his new political following, or to give an effective worker an income that would permit him to do vital but unpaid political chores is unclear. But, on 26 March 1880, this "prominent colored man in Leon County, Fla, faithful, intelligent, and competent for the duties of his office" was nominated for the position, which paid $750 annually. To sweeten the appointment, the Treasury Department provided for his accommodations in St. Marks—suggesting he did not move his family from Tallahassee—and permitted him to operate a restaurant and to carry on a freight and passenger transportation business on the side.[25]

The deputy collector chose not to move his family because it had grown and he had only recently purchased his homestead. Carrol was born in 1877, and Letty (probably Lydia) was born the next year. They lived just to the northwest of the city limits on the road that led to Bainbridge, Georgia. Proctor had purchased the ten acre plot in 1879, and it would be his home until his death. It is best described as modest: the one-story frame dwelling was a simple structure, and the land surrounding it was for basic family needs not for agriculture.[26]

Proctor served two years in St. Marks. It was not a major port of entry, and the duties could not have been arduous. He remembered it as the best position of his life. Nothing in the records stands out about his tenure. Some minor corrections from his supervisor at Cedar Key in the initial months of the job suggest he was still learning the rules. On the other side of the ledger, his name was mentioned in very positive fashion in a report to Secretary Sherman.[27]

As John entered upon his duties, presidential—and gubernatorial—politics were far advanced. The first test came in

May at the congressional nominating convention in Talla-hassee. There, Postmaster Stewart of Tallahassee led the old Wallace-Proctor pro-black faction to nominate the black George Washington Witherspoon (opposed by old foe Malachi Martin) and to endorse Grant for the presidency. Conover, seeing his Sherman hopes evaporating, supported Wither-spoon.

At the state convention later that month blacks were again in the majority. All the old wounds were still bleeding, and stanching them was no easy task. The old line Ring delegates— who backed the wrong candidate, James G. Blaine for presi-dent—supported William Ledwith; black belt carpetbaggers (generally white persons) backed Dennis Eagan; and blacks, remembering their traditional loyalties and his support of Witherspoon, pumped for Conover. Conover won (even though the convention backed Grant) but indicated his will-ingness to be open-minded by accepting the Ring candidate William Ledwith for lieutenant governor.[28] The apparent party unity did not extend to Leon County, where the old division caused its usual hardship. After multiple tickets were nominated (not including John Wallace or Deputy Collector Proctor), the regular Republican ticket, led by Julius Ball, triumphed.[29]

Florida Democrats nominated their native born and best candidate, William Bloxham, and for the first time since 1867 felt free to demonstrate their honest sentiments. They were confident, the army was gone, and they were in a majority: "For a white man to vote the Republican ticket to-day is to virtually declare to the world that he thinks the white people of Florida are not fit to rule themselves, and the reins of government should be turned over to the negroes," declared Charles Dyke. "The negroes have drawn the color line for them-selves and no white man who has any pride of character will cross over to them." And they did not. Even though Simon Conover carried Leon County (2,829 to Bloxham's 998), he lost the election statewide (23,297 to Bloxham's 28,378). In the legislature, the Republicans were in serious trouble with only five senators and seventeen assemblymen. As one student of

Florida politics put it, with the election of 1880 the "clock was turned back."[30]

Conover and the Republican party were finished in Florida politics. In a two year period the white carpetbagger had lost elections for the United States Senate, for the United States House of Representatives, and for governor of Florida—and his candidate had lost the Republican nomination for president. He was an unlikely champion of blacks in Florida, but he had been honestly and effectively just that and in a very singular sense. On 14 March 1882 John Proctor was removed as deputy collector.[31] Now he was alone.

But the waning of the Republican party did not signal acceptance of Democratic rule. Many whites in Florida (and the South) did not share the Bourbon dream of white, oligarchical direction of society and government. One of the earliest, and easily the most prominent of these was David S. Walker, Jr., son of the early Reconstruction governor. Walker had seen his brother appointed to West Point by Senator Conover and had flirted with coalition and fusion politics in Tallahassee municipal elections. In October 1881, dissatisfied with the Democrats and unwilling to become a Republican, he published a call for a new party. Walker's call did not cause the rise of Independentism in Florida so much as it was a highly visible manifestation of a movement aborning. And as other erstwhile Democrats took up the challenge, it became clear that sizeable numbers of black leaders were unhappy with the course of the Republican party and had had heretofore no political alternatives.[32]

Florida Republicans had always been troubled by factionalism. Independentism made it even worse. To some Republicans, including some black Republicans, Independency seemed like the invitation from native whites for which they had been waiting so long. Unlike those whites who had perpetrated coalition politics but would *not* leave the Democratic party, here were native whites who would say good-bye to their traditional underpinnings. What these invited blacks did not realize—or perhaps tried to ignore—was that these attractive Independents were most often thorough-going racists simply looking for votes of any color to bolster their ambition for political leadership. A strong current of Independentism first surfaced among blacks in north Florida in the late spring at an Emancipation Day meeting of blacks from Leon and Jefferson counties. Senator Conover was present and argued against the new movement. John Wallace, although respectful of Conover, counseled otherwise. Proctor, now returned from St. Marks, was probably present, although no list of participants survives.[33]

At the Leon County Republican convention in late June, the debate erupted with fury. Although Simon Conover, still active, pleaded with the delegates to remain true to their Republican ways, Senator Wallace and Postmaster Stewart openly led in the direction of the new movement. John Proctor was a delegate, but, when asked, he declined appointment to the Committee on Resolutions. Evidently he had either not yet decided whether he should break with Conover or Wallace and Stewart, or he was not ready to reveal his position. In any case, the majority of Leon County blacks signaled they were open to the new combination. "The preservation of our rights," they declared in the convention's resolutions, "requires that we should hold ourselves in readiness to give our united and solid support in favor of any movement" devoted to establishing them. The party of Lincoln, it seemed, might not fill the bill.[34]

Two months later a group of Republican leaders, seeing that party division would again insure their defeat, consulted at Quincy in order to prevent a disastrous congressional nominating convention in September. Conover, who was present, ostensibly withdrew his objections to Independentism, and the meeting disbanded after participants agreed to vote for Daniel McKinnon, erstwhile Democrat, as the fusion candidate for the nomination.

When the convention met on 5 September 1882, it was evenly divided between straight-out and pro-independent Republicans and, as usual, two sets of delegates from Leon County attended.[35] Former governor Stearns, traditional Conover-Proctor foe, led the Independent forces and recognized the Leon County delegation led by defecting Postmaster Stewart rather than the Conover crowd. That was not, however, a precursor to the nomination that the straight-out Republican candidate, Emory F. Skinner, won by three votes. A rump gathering (including David Walker, Jr., Postmaster Stewart, John Wallace, and Nicholas Eppes from Leon County and Marcellus Stearns and Malachi Martin from Gadsden County) nominated McKinnon anyway.[36]

When Leon County Republicans returned home and held their own convention, it was evident that the Independent forces had been routed there. The straight-outs were in complete control—even Postmaster Stewart recanted and pledged allegiance to the Grand Old Party. And with the party regulars in control the party regulars won the prizes. John Proctor was chosen as candidate for the Florida senate. As expected, the straight-out ticket rode roughshod over all opposition in the county, and John Proctor became Senator Proctor.[37]

That election was the peak of John Proctor's public life. He defeated the white Democrat, Pat Houston—a central figure in Leon County white society and politics—by a two to one majority. John Wallace, leading the county Independent ticket, finished a poor third. With Wallace's desertion, John Proctor became the county Republican leader. He had shown his ability—and his loyalty—in his terms in the assembly and in Leon County leadership, in his life in the county, and in his devotion to the Republican party. His nomination (even knowing of his likely election) was not simply a reward for his blind loyalty, rather it clearly was a recognition that in the trying times that faced black Republicans in the mid-1880s, John Proctor was fit for the challenge.

As Senator Proctor took his seat in Florida's upper house, the Bourbon Democrats were on the verge of their ultimate victory—banishing all blacks and any other political party from the arena. Despite the statewide flirtations with Independency, only one county had given the movement a majority. Republicans, who saw some gains over the previous election, carried only eight of the state's thirty-nine counties. The Florida senate, thirty-two senators and twenty-three committees of five members each, did not welcome Proctor. The mathematics suggested each senator should have three or four assignments. John Proctor was appointed to only one committee: Militia. Since the militia was a white organization, the message was clear—he was not of any importance. Likewise, during the course of the session, he was not appointed to any select committee. Reputation, integrity, and experience to the contrary, he would not play a significant role in this white, Democratic deliberative body.[38]

His role in the senate showed great change from his previous activity in the assembly. Now, although faithful in attendance and usually voting with the majority, his daily participation was limited, almost exclusively, to casting his vote. He made no motions to help conduct the flow of business; he rarely spoke. In the lower house he had been a real member. In every term he had either been part of the leadership or closely related to the leadership. In the senate he was a shadow member; he was a black in an age and place that was quickly and joyfully returning to white supremacy. He was his father's son: both had entered their fifth decade by losing to white society's racial matrix.

The leadership appears to have regarded Proctor without malice. He introduced five measures for the senate's consideration. Two of them, local bills, passed routinely, the others (all of which dealt with constitutional revision, the main business of the session) died in committee. Interestingly, a measure came before the legislature for some special compensation for Matthew Lively—John Proctor's former master. Although Proctor voted for the bill, confirming his positive regard for Lively, he was not its sponsor—whether he did not wish to introduce it or was denied the opportunity is unknown.[39]

The only roadblock left on the Democrats' journey to white supremacy was the Reconstruction constitution of 1868 still in effect. Full of measures designed to encourage and protect black participation in politics, it had not stopped white Democrats from taking control, but it had been from time to time inhibiting. Taking the appropriate steps to "revise"—that is to say rewrite—that constitution became the most important issue of the session. It was a foregone conclusion that constitutional revision would occur, the only issue was how and when. Senator Proctor, undoubtedly realizing the issue at stake, opposed the majority in authorizing a general constitutional convention that would give the white Democrats carte blanche to rewrite the entire document rather than more narrowly defined parts of it.[40] He, and the handful of others who voted with him, failed, and a convention bill passed.

The Leon County Republican party's fate, and John Proctor's with it, was settled in the next year. Weakened by twenty years of internal bickering and almost a decade of violence, intimidation, and fraud at the hands of Florida Democrats, the state party looked to the Independents for sustenance. The new party was so flawed, however, that it could not survive, let alone fulfill its promise. Leon County Republicans followed the state party into the abyss.

The initial move came with a meeting of black Republican leaders in Gainesville 5 February. Under the leadership of Josiah Walls, the meeting passed resolutions asking for protection of civil rights and called for Florida blacks to support an independent Democrat for governor. And, although white, black, pro- and anti-Independent Republicans were able to agree among themselves in May long enough to choose delegates to the Republican national convention, the move to Independentism in Florida continued unchecked. It was complete by the time of the state convention in July. Despite efforts of white Republicans to prevent it, the black delegates (responding to Josiah Walls's and John Wallace's urging) declined to nominate a Republican gubernatorial candidate, which left the way open for them to support the Independent candidate, Frank Pope.[41]

In Leon County that fall, a full fusion assembly ticket appeared out of the factious Republican convention. It was split between the forces. David Walker and E.C. Weeks (white, Proctor opponents) were at the top, and Clinton Snead and Samuel Frazier (blacks from the Proctor wing) provided the balance. There was no senate nominee since Proctor's term did not end for another two years. Despite Democratic victories at the national and state level, the Fusion ticket carried Leon County.[42]

The election was a disaster for Republicans, especially in Florida. A Democrat won the White House for the first time since the Civil War and Florida Democrats continued their dominance in Tallahassee. Independency, defeated at the polls, collapsed, and the blacks who had supported it were the biggest losers. They had fatally wounded the Republican party and then been cast adrift by the whites returning to the Democracy. Now Senator Proctor was even more isolated. Few Republicans untainted with Independentism were left in 1885, especially in the legislature. Despite that, or perhaps because of it, Proctor did slightly better in the session. He got two committee assignments, Militia and Public Printing. With Public Printing as with Militia, no danger existed that a lone black Republican could accomplish anything, but at least John had gained a second committee. More significantly, he was appointed to a select committee of three to visit the convict camps—an issue of importance.[43]

But John did little. In fact, as in the previous session, Leon County bills were generally handled by non-Leon County senators—a relief bill for B.C. Lewis (one of John's mentors from the 1860s) included. Proctor was one of a very small minority of five who were clearly out of sympathy with the majority. He introduced only one measure for the senate's consideration during the entire session.

The legislative session that year was really only a sideshow to the constitutional convention in mid-summer. Senator Proctor appears to have not been involved. At the Leon County Republican convention, the interloper David Walker counseled "a conciliatory policy" with the Democrats involving a split ticket. Simon Conover responded that the delegates were still Republicans and that they should act like it. His sentiments carried the day but Walker, Conover, and three blacks won the nominations and represented the county at the convention. The document that resulted confirmed white conservative control of Florida and remained in effect until 1968.[44]

The conclusion to the drama came in the fall of 1886. Leon County Republicans held at least three conventions followed by two or three private meetings. John Wallace, returning to the black Republican fold, counseled a straight-out ticket, but the Walker crowd was more numerous and led the way to a ticket based on Independentism, even though it had no state-wide basis. Left behind by that maneuver, Wallace and Proctor tried to revive their old coalition with Leon County white Democrats. The *Floridian*, even without Charles Dyke, liked that idea, but could not sell it to the local party. In the end, Leon County voters had three tickets to choose from: the Independent ticket (though it was not referred to by that name) headed by Walker, a white Democratic ticket, and a black Republican ticket (which included Wallace and Proctor as candidates for the Assembly). Proctor and his comrades finished a very distant third.[45] The Florida Republican party, and John Proctor, had no political future left.

TEN

Afterword

Letty Proctor was born in 1878. Very late in her life she recalled that the earliest memory she had of her father's occupation was of his being a mason. He laid bricks for the rest of his life, she confirmed, and, "Oh blessed be, he was laying brick when he died."[1] The importance of Letty's statement was not in identifying her father's occupation, for that was common knowledge, but the timing of it. John Proctor's last legislative service was in 1886, the year his youngest daughter turned eight.

Senator Proctor did not arbitrarily decide to leave public life and change careers. Rather, the conditions that made possible, indeed impelled, his political career, had changed rapidly. Reconstruction was finished—not completed but failed. Any disposition to be open-minded about racial attitudes—or any other fundamental ideas about Southern life—was rapidly disappearing, if, indeed, they had ever been sincerely questioned. By the mid-1880s, the *Floridian* (under its new editors) revealed its attitude about the black population's potential and place in society by complaining that because "colored people [were] leaving" the area, there would be a great scarcity of good house servants and farm laborers. Still the editors continued to provide news coverage of black persons in a neutral tone. The newspaper chronicled the opening of a roller skating rink and the first hotel built for "colored persons" and enthusiastically supported plans for the "first annual assembly of the National Colored Chautauqua," noting it would bring "prominent and highly educated colored men" to Tallahassee.[2]

The great change came quickly. In 1892 a leading Tallahassee hotel announced it had hired white waitresses and done away with "the unreliable colored waiters"—meaning all black waiters and not just those who were deficient. A decade later the "white only" establishment had become commonplace, and racial attitudes rapidly deteriorated to the point where the editor was incensed about the "incident" that resulted when a black person would not give way to a white person on the sidewalk.[3]

The magnitude of coming change was not evident in 1886, but its beginnings were clear. And while the shift to overt racism was making itself felt generally, there were particularly distressing circumstances for citizen Proctor. The likelihood of political relief was dim; electoral and administrative office appeared out of the question. Neither was there any realistic expectation of assistance in the private sector. Conover, Dyke, and their lieutenants no longer had positions of prominence; the circumstances of the Lewis and Lively relief bills showed the connection with childhood patrons had been effectively broken, and Proctor had no replacements for these powerful friends and patrons. The prospect was probably chilling. John had six children at home, and he, who had no real career apart from politics, was out of office. Had he wanted to farm, he did not own enough land (only ten acres) to do anything but provide a household garden, and there was no evidence of any livestock or, in fact, any agricultural production. Money was scarce. In 1889, the Proctors, who owned their land free and clear, mortgaged it.[4]

Unlike many black persons of his era, John Proctor had never seen land ownership as a means to security. Neither had he learned and practiced a trade. He had placed his reliance on politics, and when that was gone his alternatives were severely limited. He did not have capital available for starting a business (as he had done in St. Marks), and he evidently rejected schoolteaching. Instead he turned to bricklaying. This new way of life was probably difficult for him. He was forty-two

years old and, while he had tasted the rewards of success—
limited in his case to public acclaim and not including, evidently, material reward—it had been taken from him. He
experienced some bitterness.[5] But he came to accept the reality of the situation and turned to earning a living for his family.
As a bricklayer citizen Proctor did not retreat into a shell.
He continued his involvement in Leon County politics. He was
realist enough to have known that there was no possibility of
winning. But fragmentary evidence indicates that he continued to speak in support of civil rights for black persons and
to uphold the right of participation in local politics.[6] He occupied a position of significance in the local black hierarchy.
For unknown reasons he left the Methodist church and in 1887
joined a group of black worthies (including the president of
what became Florida A & M University) to found St. Michaels
and All Angels Episcopal Church. Church records refer to him
as "Senator" Proctor. He was a sought-after pallbearer and
groomsman for the town's black population and remained
concerned and involved with Tallahassee's black schools.[7]

Little other information survives concerning the next forty
years of John's life. His economic status is evident from tax and
land records. He maintained a modest existence and never
really achieved financial security. After 1890 he only occasionally owned a horse, and the tax assessor consistently identified
only minimal personal property. After satisfying the 1889
mortgage in 1894, Proctor mortgaged his property again later
the same year. This mortgage must have been satisfied, for the
land was again obligated in 1915. That mortgage was cleared in
1923.[8] He never acquired additional real property.

Some details about the immediate family are known.
Mary died sometime between 1880 and 1899. That year John remarried. His bride was Malinda, who had come to the United
States in 1894 from St. Vincent and was some fifteen years
younger than him. Evidently he would later enter a third
marriage, this one to Martha Littleton in 1916. Martha died
prior to 1934.[9]

For some of the children the record is clear. The younger
John took as his wife Maggie and sometime around 1890 built

his home next to his father's. He bought the property in 1910. Julia married John Rollins in 1894; the new couple would acquire part of the original ten-acre Proctor homestead in the late 1930s. For Henrietta the record is not available; she was not living with her father and stepmother in 1900. Mary may have been the wife of Willie Carr. If this is the case, then that couple also acquired a portion of the old homestead in 1935. Carrol married and produced a family; he acquired a portion of the family place in 1937. Lettie married Samuel Hill in 1905. That union produced one daughter. Lettie survived both her husband and her child and, at some point, returned to her father's home to care for him. She died there in 1978. Matthew Proctor, of whom little is known, was not a part of the household.[10]

Plenty of extended family lived in the vicinity. John's brothers, George and Bahamia, saw the way to the future in acquiring and working land. George, who had served one term in the legislature, and his wife Louisa had seven children by 1900 and owned over three hundred acres of land in the county that they actively farmed. George may have maintained contact with surviving Proctors in St. Augustine, for at least three of his children, Martha, Florida, and Henry, returned there. Bahamia seems to have remained all his life with the Finlayson family in Jefferson County. By 1900 his and Juda's family was complete with six children, the last of whom was sixteen at the time. Shortly they would own at least a hundred acres of land that they too actively farmed.[11] The rest of George and Nancy's children had passed from public view.

At some point John Proctor became too old to lay bricks, Letty's comment to the contrary. By then he was becoming part of the local pantheon. At the 1924 Tallahassee Centennial Celebration he was accorded a place of honor on the capitol platform and treated courteously and kindly during the ceremony. Because he had outlived most of his contemporaries, he was regarded by the community and persons interested in the past as a local sage. The state librarian, W.T. Cash, consulted him regularly, and he seems to have had a regular procession of visitors, including many white patricians, who stopped by his home on Old Bainbridge Road. He generally walked to town and back each day and seems to have divided his church attendance (Episcopalian) between St. Michael's (black) and St. John's (white).

Like his grandfather, John remained mentally acute. He read newspapers regularly and was well informed—and opinionated—on current events. His reading extended beyond journalism to book-length material and the Bible. On at least six occasions during the last decade of his life he gave long interviews, and the results of those depended upon the sensitivity and open-mindedness of the interviewer. At least one of the interviewers was black.

John Proctor died on 15 December 1944 at the age of one hundred years and eleven months. He had been out of public life for half a century. He had seen all those issues he fought for disappear. Civil rights, including voting, economic opportunity, schools—all had been withdrawn or made inferior. Contrary to their wishes, black political leaders had been replaced by the apolitical, self-help doctrines of the Booker Washington variety. That had not worked either.

The experiences of the three Proctor men reflected in a real way the history of black persons in American society. Toney, the soldier, had prospered in an age of equality following the American revolution. But the rise of the cotton kingdom and the tightening bonds of a slavery system justified on the grounds of black inferiority had doomed entrepreneur George. Politician John's career followed closely the course of Reconstruction, and he too, was defeated by color.

All the three Proctor men would have taken comfort that within twenty-one years of John's passing, the United States Supreme Court decisively brought to an end the governmental imprimatur that had controlled and negated their lives. From what we know of them, it is likely that they would have believed their experiences, and their lives, were given new meaning at that instant.

Notes

LCDB   Leon County, Fla., Deed Books
LCLF   Leon County, Fla., Law Files
LCMB   Leon County, Fla., Mortgage Books
LCOR   Leon County, Fla., Official Records
LCTR   Leon County, Fla., Tax Rolls
SJCDB   St. Johns County, Fla., Deed Books
TCDB   Tuolumne County, Calif., Deed Books

1. ANTONIO THE SOLDIER

1. Most of what is known of Antonio Proctor's life is based, in one way or another, on the single personal document that survives: his obituary. Published in the *Tallahassee Sentinel* 3 July 1855, it was the only known instance of a black person's death (and life) so chronicled in Tallahassee prior to the Civil War. Sympathetic and admiring in tone, it was written by Benjamin F. Allen, Whig editor of the paper, Florida's secretary of state 1863-1868, and a friend of the Proctor family. It was based on an intimate knowledge of the man and his life. The birthplace and Spanish surname are explicitly confirmed in Langhorne's interview with John Proctor. The *Sentinel* obituary says he was born in Jamaica.

2. Antonio signed his legal documents with an "X." See, for example, SJCDB E:91, LCLF 170.

3. It is unlikely that Antonio ever crossed the Atlantic; surely

there would have been some reference to such an event had it occurred.

4. The discussion of the background and operations of Panton, Leslie and Company is drawn from Coker, "Entrepreneurs," 18-22.

5. Tebeau, *History of Florida*, 73-89.

6. Allen, "A Natural Death." Many parts of this obituary must be considered Antonio's own testimony, since only he could have made the obscure parts of his life known.

7. A. Proctor [Claim], American State Papers 4:159, 177, Report 1, No. 211 (Descriptive List N. 256), ms. in Bureau of Land Records, Department of Natural Resources, Tallahassee, Florida; DuVal statement in petition of Antonio Proctor; Harvey, "Antonio Proctor," 51; SJCDB I-J:13.

8. Allen, "A Natural Death."

9. Porter, "Negroes and East Florida Annexation," 18-9; "Talk of Tuskegee Tustumugee," 182. There is documentary evidence that Antonio served as an Indian interpreter for the Americans. There is no evidence as to how or when he learned the Indian's language. See note 21, below.

10. Porter, "Negroes and East Florida Annexation," 20-21.

11. American State Papers 4: 159, 177, Report 1, No. 211 (Descriptive list no. 256).

12. Cathedral Parish Records, Colored Baptisms, 1807-1848 (Reel #3), St. Augustine Historical Society, quoted in Harvey, "Antonio Proctor," 51.

13. Ibid. Professor Michael Scardaville aided immensely in my understanding of Spanish St. Augustine.

14. Jordan, "American Chiaroscuro," 184-89.

15. D.B. Davis, *Problem of Slavery*, 273-81. See also McAlister, *Spain and Portugal*, 418-422.

16. *San Francisco Elevator*, 15 Jan. 1869.

17. SJCDB I-J:13.

18. Garvin, "Free Negro in Florida Before the Civil War," 1-7, 9.

19. Smith, *Slavery and Plantation Growth*, 113.

20. Escritura, East Florida Papers, bundle 364, no. 10, fols. 414-17. Professor Scardaville located this document.

21. *Territorial Papers of the United States*, 23:141-44; DuVal statement in petition of Antonio Proctor.

22. Harvey, "Antonio Proctor," 52.

23. SJCDB E:91; *Ex Parte George Proctor, a minor* v. *Daniel McQuaig*, LCLF 170.

24. SJCDB I-J:13, LCDB C:490; *Ex Parte George Proctor.*

2. GEORGE THE ENTREPRENEUR

1. Murat, *Moral and Political Sketch,* 44.
2. Population schedules for Leon County, Fla., Fifth U.S. Census (1830), 1-8, and Sixth U.S. Census (1840), 76-81.
3. Paisley, *From Cotton to Quail,* 1-14.
4. Groene, *Antebellum Tallahassee,* 41-47, provides a convenient reference for settlers' starting points. On the matter of being Episcopalian, see St. John's "Parish Register."
5. Charles Hutchinson to ?, 1 Sept. 1840, quoted in Campbell, "Charles Hutchinson Letters," 16-17.
6. Abbey, "Lafayette," 1-9.
7. Fifth U.S. Census (1830), population schedules for Leon County, Fla., 1-8.
8. "Cousin Ann" to Martha Bradford, 5 June 1832, Pine Hill Plantation Papers; *Tallahassee Floridian,* 16 Aug. 1834, 8 June 1833, 17 July, 7 Aug., 14 Aug., 16 Oct. 1841; *Tallahassee Sentinel,* 22 Oct. 1841.
9. *Tallahassee Floridian,* 27 June 1830, 6 Feb. 1836, 22 Sept. 1838, 9 Jan. 1847, 3 Oct. 1857; *Star of Florida,* 18 Apr. 1845.
10. *Star of Florida,* 27 May, 1 June 1843.
11. For a convenient chronicle of the violence, see Groene, *Antebellum Tallahassee,* 99-103.
12. Castlenau, "Essay on Middle Florida," 237; Tappan to "My very dear cousin " 109
13. Berlin, *Slaves Without Masters,* 247.
14. LCDB A:222-25, 232, 488; E:64, 211; F:50; G:158 are all typical examples.
15. *Florida Watchman,* 6 Jan. 1838. The issue is misdated 1837.
16. LCLF 170.
17. LCDB E:331.
18. LCDB E:607.
19. On this point see Curry, *Free Black in Urban America,* xix.
20. Florida, *Journal of Eleventh Session,* 42. There were three persons on the committee, two from Leon County. For the measure to have died, at least one of the two had to oppose it.
21. LCDB E:66, 113-14, 140, 775, 797, 801; F:154.
22. Parker, "The Proctors," 22.
23. LCDB E:590, 787; G:377; I:605; K:166, 277. Leon County Probate File, 67, 477.

24. Examination of the extant LCTR suggests that Proctor was the only black to pay a white poll tax. On the legal status of free blacks, see, in addition to Berlin's *Slaves Without Masters*, Smith, *Slavery and Plantation Growth*, 112-15, 119-21. See also Thomas, "Free Negro in Florida before 1865," 335-45; Garvin, "Free Negro in Florida Before the Civil War," 1-17. For treatment of a free black in the Upper South and Midwest, see Walker, *Free Frank*.

25. Parker, "The Proctors," 25. Examination of federal census records suggests that other free blacks and mulattoes may have had these "guardians." At least they appear to have been recorded with white households. Proctor's likely immunity no doubt sprang from the "privileges, rights and immunities" to be maintained in the 1819 treaty with Spain. George's son confirmed the guardian requirement but named none for his father. He did say Henry Rutgers was his "agent." Unknown is whether that meant Rutgers was acting in a business capacity for George or whether it meant that Rutgers was his guardian. Langhorne's interview with John Proctor.

26. My analysis of the power and politics is taken from Thomason, *Jackson Democracy*, especially 3-22; and Doherty, *Whigs*, especially 5-29.

27. Doherty, *Call*, does not mention Proctor. This is not in itself strange since they lived close to each other, and whatever contacts they might have had would probably have been oral. "Old Governor Call," as John called him, knew Toney from the Seminole war days. A patronlike relationship with George could logically have followed from that experience

28. LCDB E:801; F:154; H:379.

29. LCDB E:66; G:695; LCLF 2754, 3141, 3279, 3499.

30. LCDB G:569; H:374; I:384; *Tallahassee Sentinel*, 8 Apr. 1842.

31. DuVal was later known as a Democrat. LCDB H:397; LCLF 5256.

32. Transactions with Romeo Lewis include LCDB E:381, C:489 and G:569. For cases with Westcott as attorney, see LCLF 2867, 3279, 3284, 3354, 3690, 3820, 3960, 4188.

33. Berlin, *Slaves without Masters*, 247, 341-42.

34. For another free black entrepreneur's experience see Walker, *Free Frank*, 62-65.

3. WORK AND FAMILY

1. Dodd, "Corporation of Tallahassee," 86.

2. *Star of Florida*, 24 May 1844.

3. Dodd, "Old Tallahassee," 68. See also, *Star of Florida*, 22 Nov. 1844.

4. His masonry houses were the Chaires mansion and the Randall-Lewis house. The frame dwellings included the "three sisters" on Park between Gadsden and Meridian (destroyed prior to 1900), the house at 101 NA (destroyed), the house on 28-29 SA (destroyed), the Maxwell house at Bel Aire (destroyed, probably, before 1900), the house at 222 OP (moved and extant), and the Rutgers house.

5. For one analysis of wood content, see R.C. Koepen, Center for Wood Anatomy, to Curtis E. Peterson, 5 Nov. 1975; Curtis E. Peterson to author, 17 Nov. 1975, Historic Tallahassee Preservation Board.

6. For a brief analysis of a Proctor dwelling, see Eastland and Anthony, *Randall-Lewis House*.

7. LCDB H:397.

8. LCDB G:158; K:48, 99; I:232; LCTR, 1847-1851.

9. Obviously many other factors were involved in their survival.

10. LCDB G:272.

11. LCDB F:494.

12. LCLF 2242, 2968; LCDB K:19.

13. LCLF 5374.

14. By 1850, out of a total black population in Tallahassee of 778, forty-one were free. Of these, eight were adult males capable of physical labor.

15. LCTR, 1845-1848. Sixth U.S. Census (1840), population schedules for Leon County, Fla., 50.

16. LCLF 3354, 3499, 3820; LCDB I:384. Proctor was by no means unique in the practice: Antonio had owned a slave. See also Franklin, "James Boon," 150-80.

17. LCLF 482.

18. LCDB E:590, G:569, H:397; *Tallahassee Sentinel* 8 Apr. 1842.

19. For typical examples, see LCLF 5446 (Proctor as debtor) or LCLF 2869 (Proctor as creditor).

20. See LCDB E:590; LCLF 2526, 3254, 3944, 4188.

21. Parochial Register, 1832-1913, St. John's Episcopal Church.

22. LCDB G:155. A careful student of the local slave economy called the $1,300 price "unusually high." Paisley, *Red Hills*, 182. Several times John identified James Lockaman as Nancy's owner and, on one occasion, said she was twice purchased. Lockaman at different times had liens on Mrs. Chandler's house, some of the property of her second husband, and, potentially, some joint property. The mortgage

on Nancy may have passed along this chain. See Langhorne's interview with John Proctor; LCDB E:625; I:151.
    23. Parochial Register, 1832-1913, St. John's Episcopal Church; Sixth U.S. Census (1840), population schedules for Leon County, Fla., 50. John said his younger brother's name was Bahamia, given to him by Antonio. Langhorne's interview with John Proctor.
    24. Parochial Register, 1832-1913, St. John's Episcopal Church; LCDB H:374; LCLF 3844.
    25. *Tallahassee Sentinel*, 3 July 1855; Parker, "The Proctors," 26.

4. REVERSAL

    1. My discussion of the panic and the depression is taken from Temin, *Jacksonian Economy*, 113-79; on Tallahassee, see *Star of Florida*, 22 May, 22 Nov. 1844.
    2. See Doherty, *Call*, 109-11; Groene, *Antebellum Tallahassee*, 47-50; *Star of Florida*, 22 May 1844.
    3. DuVal went bankrupt himself. *Tallahassee Sentinel*, 11 Nov. 1842.
    4. LCLF 2476, 3144, 3145.
    5. LCLF 2526, 2754, 2968, 3120, 2482.
    6. LCLF 2869, 3499.
    7. LCLF 3120, 3194, 3279, 3284, 3254, 3820, 3944, 4188. These suits were not filed until 1842, but they were all for notes that came due some months before the date of filing.
    8. LCLF 3141.
    9. Ibid.
    10. Ibid.
    11. LCLF 2526, 2754, 2968, 3120.
    12. LCLF 3482. This file is unusually full, containing material, bills, and interrogatories that supply much information about Proctor and Tallahassee.
    13. LCLF 4690.
    14. LCLF 3354.
    15. LCLF 3284.
    16. LCLF 3194.
    17. LCLF 3960.
    18. LCLF 3020, 3279, 3820, 4188. There was no award in *Albertson v. Proctor* because of the plaintiff's death. Evidently his heirs did not press the suit.

19. There is no biography of Westcott. See Doherty, *Call,* 76, 78, 82-3, 110, 120, 128, 146.
20. LCLF 4690.
21. LCLF 2869.
22. LCLF 3499.
23. LCLF 5407.
24. LCDB I:103-104, K:18, 19. *Tallahassee Sentinel,* 4 Feb.; 25 Mar.; 8, 15, 29 Apr. 1842.
25. *Tallahassee Sentinel,* 4 Feb. 1842.
26. LCDB G:569, H:397. Brady, "Relative Prices in the Nineteenth Century," 160-63, provides helpful statistics on house prices.
27. On the 40 foot by 30 foot house, see LCDB F:494.
28. Leon County Minute Book 5:599.

5. GEORGE'S DEFEAT

1. Parker, "The Proctors," 24.
2. LCDB H:374.
3. LCDB I:348.
4. Leon County Minute Book 5:599.
5. Leon County Execution and Judgment Docket, book 1. John Taylor, Mary's new husband, had his own financial problems, which may have influenced Mary's disposition of the execution. See LCDB I:151.
6. Senate Committee on Indian Affairs, "Affidavit of Toney Proctor, 4 Apr. 1848," in *Memorial of the Governor,* 30th Cong, 1st sess.
7. Senate Committee on Indian Affairs, W. Medill to Thomas Douglass, 14 June 1847, and James McCall to W. Medill, 12 June 1847, 30th Cong., 1st sess.
8. White, *Jacksonians,* 157-62.
9. LCDB I:348.
10. LCDB I:122.
11. See LCLF 5374, which contains a check to Rutgers.
12. LCTR, 1840-1850; Parker, "The Proctors," 22.
13. LCLF 5374.
14. Ibid.
15. *Tallahassee Sentinel,* 27 June 1848.
16. At least there was no further mention of it.
17. The Bryant suit was over one of Proctor's notes from 1840. As such he must have known it was coming, and it does not, in any case,

represent a failure of a new enterprise. LCLF 5336, 5256; Leon County Minute Book 5:130.
    18. Leon County Minute Book 5:151.
    19. *Floridian and Journal*, 10 Mar. 1849. This is one of but two surviving pieces of Proctor's direct thought or writing.
    20. Bartlett, *New Country*, 108-109.
    21. *Floridian*, 6 June 1849 (misdated?). George's granddaughter believed he had gone "with" the Bartlett party. See Lettie [Proctor] Hill, oral history interview. John agreed. See Langhorne's interview with John Proctor. It is possible that Proctor and the Bartlett party were together on the journey from Tallahassee to New Orleans, the first leg of the trip. At that point, it is clear, they took different routes.
    22. Ibid.
    23. LCLF 5374.
    24. Parochial Register, 1832-1913, St. John's Episcopal Church.

6. CALIFORNIA

    1. *Daily Picayune*, 12, 14, 16, 17 Apr. 1849; Haskins, *Argonauts of California*, 478.
    2. Lapp, *Blacks in Gold Rush California*, 21, 39.
    3. His son would find a similar environment in Reconstruction Tallahassee.
    4. Ibid., 186.
    5. TCDB 1:173. The deed does not identify "Proctor and Co." further.
    6. Gudde, *California Gold Camps*, 327-28. This reference also contains a contemporary print of Sonora.
    7. Christman, *One Man's Gold*, 197-98. The date of the entry is 9 August 1851.
    8. Seventh U.S. Census (1850), population schedules for Tuolumne County, Calif., 181; Buckbee, *Saga of Old Tuolumne*, 558. Buckbee lists Proctor as one of the pioneers (516), but does not mention him in the text.
    9. TCDB 1:238-9.
    10. TCDB 1:236.
    11. Allen, "A Natural Death." Recordings of John Proctor's reminiscences, cited in note 23, agree that some money, or gold, was received.
    12. TCDB A:10, 605.
    13. Lapp, *Blacks in Gold Rush California*, 79.

14. *Sonora Herald,* 3 Feb., 30 Nov., 7 Dec., 14 Dec., 21 Dec. 1850, 19 Apr., 20 Sept. 1851.

15. TCDB 1:265, 675-76.

16. TCDB A:10, 605.

17. Tuolumne County Tax Roll, 1852; *Sonora Herald,* 4 Dec. 1852.

18. *Sonora Herald,* Steamer Issue, 1 July 1852.

19. Tuolumne County Judgment Docket B; *Sonora Herald,* 4 Dec. 1852.

20. TCDB A:10, 208-209.

21. One John Proctor reminiscence noted a rumor that he spent some time in Mexico. J. Proctor, Black Archives, 3.

22. Gudde, *California Gold Camps,* 328.

23. *Sonora Herald,* 4 Dec. 1852.

24. Parker, "The Proctors," 25. The matter of correspondence is addressed in two other accounts of the oral tradition. See Palmer, "The Proctors," 15; and J. Proctor, Federal Writers' Project, 1. Nancy could not write or read, so someone had to fulfil that function for her. John, the sole source of the oral tradition, was but four at the time of George's departure and nine at the time of the family's sale, so he may not be the best witness as to the volume or frequency of letters. And, as his later actions would show, he may have had substantial resentment of his father leading him to minimize George's communication. Nancy's illiteracy is confirmed in the 1870 census.

25. LCDB K:672. At the time he left for California, Proctor had four outstanding debts: $643 to James Bryant; $1,023 (subject to later credits) to Mary Chandler; an uncertain sum (probably around $400) to Ellen Vass; and $232.26 to T. and R. Hayward. Leon County Minute Book 5:599.

26. Allen, "A Natural Death."

27. *San Francisco Elevator,* 15 Jan. 1869.

28. Leon County Minute Book 5:599.

29. See, for example, TCDB 10:208-209, 610, 738-39.

30. *San Francisco Elevator,* 15 Jan. 1869.

31. See, for example, *Sonora Herald,* 1 Mar. 1856.

32. Lapp, *Blacks in Gold Rush California,* especially 196, 222, 256. See also *Columbia Gazette & Southern Mines Advertiser,* 17 Nov. 1855.

33. *San Francisco Elevator,* 30 Oct. 1868.

34. Ibid., 1 Nov. 1867.

35. Ibid.

36. Tuolumne County Inquest, no. 22.

37. Tuolumne County Transcript of Judgment Book 2:46-47.

38. TCDB A:10:605.

39. Tuolumne County Judgment Docket C; Tuolumne County Judgment Book C:342-43.

40. One John Proctor reminiscence noted a rumor that George had married a Mexican woman. J. Proctor, Black Archives, 3.

41. Sonora City Burial Record, 13-14; *San Francisco Elevator*, 15 Jan. 1869.

7. GEORGE'S FAMILY

1. Seventh U.S. Census (1850), population schedules for Leon County, Fla., 424. (Enumeration of household made June 1, 1850.)

2. In the second generation of known births there were two Georges, two Johns, a Toney and two Floridas. Nancy and George's firstborn had been Florida, who died shortly after birth. A Nancy does appear in the third generation.

3. Parker, "The Proctors," 24.

4. Seventh U.S. Census (1850) for Leon County, Fla., 424; LCOR 37:112; Parker, "The Proctors," 27.

5. Langhorne's interview with John Proctor; LCDB M:211. John also said that one of his prominent white friends, Dr. Henry E. Palmer, did not like him to reveal Archer's name, suggesting there was considerable opprobrium that attached to the deed. It is reasonable to believe that Palmer's attitude was shared by others of his class and that a kind of conspiracy prevented Archer's action from being revealed in print. The Langhorne interview, never transcribed, is the sole record of the accusation.

6. *San Francisco Elevator*, 15 Jan. 1869; Leon County Minute Book 5:599; Allen, "A Natural Death."

7. LCDB L:640, M:211, 323, 375.

8. Parker, "The Proctors," 26; LCDB M:375; Paisley, *Red Hills*, 207.

9. "Freedmans Savings and Trust Company," Applications 43 (John Proctor), 887 (Charlotte Proctor), and 919 (J.E. Proctor); Ninth U.S. Census (1870), population schedules for Leon County, Fla., 672.

10. The census of 1860 recorded slaves as the property of an owner without listing any name—only age, sex, and color.

11. John's reminiscences are recorded in Parker, "The Proctors," 26-27; Palmer, "The Proctors," 14-16; J. Proctor, Federal Writers' Project; *Florida Legislature Unofficial Directory*, 34; J. Proctor, Black Archives; and Langhorne's interview.

12. "Freedmans Savings and Trust Company," Application 43 (John Proctor); Parker, "The Proctors," 26. Lettie [Proctor] Hill, oral history interview; Leon County Probate File 2910; Langhorne's interview with John Proctor.

13. John said of himself, "I used to be a bad fellow with a knife." Langhorne's interview with John Proctor.

14. J. Proctor, Federal Writers' Project, 2; Paisley, *Red Hills*, 207.

15. Discussion of the political events of 1865 is taken from Shofner, *Nor Is It Over Yet*, 38-47.

16. Shofner, *Nor Is It Over Yet*, 46; see also Wallace, *Carpet-bag Rule*, 17.

17. Shofner, *Nor Is It Over Yet*, 47-49.

18. Meador, "Florida Political Parties," 187, has a complementary view.

19. Foner, *Reconstruction*, 330-31.

20. Lamb, "John Proctor," 2; "Freedmans Savings and Trust Company," Application 43 (John Proctor); Leon County Marriage [colored] Book Y:12; Leon County Marriage [colored] Book 7:28.

21. Parker, "The Proctors," 27; Langhorne's interview with John Proctor.

22. Ninth U.S. Census (1870), population schedules for Jefferson County, Fla., 362, and for Leon County, Fla., 637; Edwin H. Finlayson to Malcomb Johnson.

23. Leon County Marriage [colored] Book Z:98; "Freedmans Savings and Trust Company," Applications 887 (Charlotte Proctor) and 919 (J.E. Proctor); Ninth U.S. Census (1870), population schedules for Leon County, Fla., 672.

8. JOHN THE POLITICIAN

1. On 20 August 1867 there were 2,620 blacks and 467 whites registered. *Tallahassee Floridian*, 23 Aug. 1867.

2. My discussion of Pearce (whose highest rank in the church was that of elder) is taken from Dodd, "'Bishop' Pearce," 5-12.

3. See Litwack, *Been in the Storm so Long*, 470-71.

4. *Tallahassee Floridian*, 3 May, 12 Nov. 1867, 29 Dec. 1868, 3 Oct. 1883; House, *Executive Documents*, 337.

5. LCOR 37:112.

6. "The ascendancy of the Democratic party to the State government in 1877," concluded the author after long experience, "has proved a blessing in disguise to the colored people of Florida." See

Wallace, *Carpet-bag Rule*, 4. See also Richardson, *Negro in the Recon-struction*, 192-93.

7. Dodd, "'Bishop' Pearce," 8.

8. *Tallahassee, Floridian*, 12 July 70. This was the first recorded notice of John Proctor.

9. *Tallahassee Floridian*, 19, 23 Apr., 7 May, 24 Sept. 1867, 2 Mar. 1869. Other white Southerners had similar experiences. See Foner, *Reconstruction*, 412.

10. *Tallahassee Floridian*, 19 May 1868, 6 July 1869, 6 Aug. 1872, 28 Sept. 1880. The ticket was endorsed by the Florida Democratic party.

11. Parker, "The Proctors," 27; "Bureau of Refugees, Freedmen and Abandoned Lands," vol. 21:57.

12. Wallace, *Carpet-bag Rule*, 155; *Tallahassee Floridian*, 6 Aug. 1872.

13. *Tallahassee Floridian*, 6 Aug. 1872.

14. Ibid., 13 Aug. 1872.

15. Ibid., 20 Aug., 27 Aug., 3 Sept. 1872.

16. Wallace, *Carpet-bag Rule*, 217; *Tallahassee Floridian*, 22 Oct. 1872.

17. Corruption, says Foner, "may be ubiquitous in American history, but it thrived in the Reconstruction South because of the specific circumstances of Republican rule." In general, whites profited substantially more than blacks, and the stain transcended party lines. Proctor clearly was not a major player—if he was a player at all. He would profit by the jobs he held when the legislature was not in session and on one occasion accepted a proffered bribe and then in a defiant, open manner, did not deliver. *Reconstruction*, 384-89.

18. Just after the election they organized a convention of Leon county agricultural laborers (Proctor signed the meeting call). *Tallahassee Floridian*, 19 Nov. 1872.

19. The vote was 28 to 20. Wallace, *Carpet-bag Rule*, 265-67, 273-74, 288; *Tallahassee Floridian*, 4 Feb. 1873.

20. Florida, *Journal of Sixth Session*, 23-24, 64, 94, 96, 122, 151, 153, 281, 245-46; Wallace, *Carpet-bag Rule*, 265-67; Jno. E. Proctor to Hon S.B. Conover, undated, "Nineteenth Century Florida State Legislature Session Documents."

21. Wallace, *Carpet-bag Rule*, 265-67.

22. Ibid., 272, 274-75; Richardson, *Negro in the Reconstruction*, 195, interprets this incident to question Proctor's "honor."

23. *Tallahassee Floridian*, 4 Feb. 1873. On the election and the

maneuvering that surrounded it, see Wallace, *Carpet-bag Rule*, 227-28, 273-74, 276, 288-89; Florida, *Journal of the Sixth Session*, 86-143.

24. Florida, *Journal of the Sixth Session*, 29-30, 58-59; Foner, *Reconstruction*, 539-41; Shofner, *Nor Is It Over Yet*, 290-91.

25. Shofner, *Nor Is It Over Yet*, 134-35, 221, 245-46, 281; *Tallahassee Floridian*, 16 Sept. 1873; Wallace, *Carpet-bag Rule*, 268, 288-89. Jonathan Gibbs was the only black to hold high state office during Reconstruction.

26. Wallace, *Carpet-bag Rule*, 227-28, 288-89; *Tallahassee Floridian*, 11 Mar., 8 July 1873.

27. *Tallahassee Floridian*, 16, 23, 30 Sept. 1873. Only a few issues of the *Tallahassee Sentinel* survive for the entire Reconstruction period. The relevant issues here are missing.

28. Florida, *Journal of the Seventh Session*, 3-7, 45-46; Wallace, *Carpet-bag Rule*, 228-29.

29. Florida, *Journal of the Seventh Session*, 291-93, 342, 344-45; Wallace, *Carpet-bag Rule*, 248-49.

30. Florida, *Journal of the Seventh Session*, 53, 67, 94, 106, 112, 160, 206-7, 230, 238, 241, 319, 346-47.

31. Foner, *Reconstruction*, 381-83; Shofner, *Nor Is It Over Yet*, 292.

32. *Tallahassee Floridian*, 14, 21, 28 July 1874. By this time Governor Hart, never physically strong, had died and was replaced by Lieutenant Governor Marcellus Stearns. Stearns, from neighboring Gadsden County, was a fierce foe of Wallace and Proctor and personally attended the reconciliation meeting.

33. The records of the election are found in "Nineteenth Century Florida State Legislature [General Assembly] Documents re: Contested elections," 1874, Box 15, Folder 7. See also *Tallahassee Floridian*, 10, 17 Nov. 1874.

34. Florida, *Journal of the Eighth Session*, 308.

35. Florida, *Journal of the Eighth Session*, 95, 109, 234-35, 238, 294, 350, 361; *Tallahassee Floridian*, 23 Feb., 2 Mar. 1875.

36. Florida, *Journal of the Eighth Session*, 238. John said that banker B.C. Lewis warned him of the coming failure, which enabled him to withdraw his own funds. The action showed Proctor had not burned his bridges to the Tallahasseeans of his youth. Parker, "The Proctors, 27.

37. Florida, *Journal of the Eighth Session*, 130, 240; *Tallahassee Floridian*, 16 Feb. 1875; Williamson, *Florida Politics*, 9.

9. The End of Reconstruction

1. Foner, *Reconstruction*, 525; Hoogenboom, *Hayes*, 6.

2. The opposition *Sentinel* identified Proctor as being from the "Democratic wing of the Republican party" and questioned his intelligence and competence for the position. See *Tallahassee Sentinel*, 14 Aug., 2 Oct. 1875; *Tallahassee Floridian*, 1 June, 17 Aug. 1875.

3. Tenth U.S. Census (1880), population schedules for Leon County, Fla., ED 88, Sheet 37; LCTR, 1874-1877. Proctor is not listed in the 1873 tax roll or any earlier extant LCTR.

4. Courtship of Democrats was not reserved to the Conover-Wallace-Proctor Republicans. There were continual efforts by Republican opponents to supplant them in the coalition. Marcellus Stearns was one who made these efforts. See Peek, "Election of 1870," 367.

5. *Tallahassee Floridian*, 24 Nov., 22 Dec. 1874, 12 Jan. 1875, 1 Jan. 1878, 4 June 1879; *Tallahassee Sentinel*, 11 Sept. 1875.

6. *Tallahassee Floridian*, 23 Nov. 1875.

7. *Tallahassee Sentinel*, 26 Feb. 1876; *Tallahassee Floridian*, 8, 22, 26 Feb. 1876. The *Floridian* had become a biweekly for the campaign.

8. *Tallahassee Sentinel*, 3, 17 June, 15 July 1876; *Tallahassee Floridian*, 2, 16 May, 6 June 1876; Wallace, *Carpet-bag Rule*, 331.

9. Wallace, *Carpet-bag Rule*, 331; *Tallahassee Sentinel*, 17 June, 15 July 1876; Klingman, *Walls*, 112.

10. *Tallahassee Sentinel*, 19 Aug., 16 Sept. 1876; *Tallahassee Floridian*, 15 Aug. 1876.

11. *Tallahassee Floridian*, 29 Aug. 1876; Wallace, *Carpet-bag Rule*, 333-34.

12. *Tallahassee Sentinel*, 21 Oct. 1876. Proctor's appointment came from a federal judge in Jacksonville.

13. Foner, *Reconstruction*, 596, 598, 882-83; Hoogenboom, *Hayes*, 60-61, 69-70.

14. *Tallahassee Floridian*, 26 June, 10 July 1877, 25 Dec. 1877. Floridians were not the only ones hearing these sentiments. See Foner, *Reconstruction*, 525, 546.

15. *Tallahassee Floridian*, 2 Oct. 1877, 5 Mar., 15, 22 Oct., 5 Nov. 1878; Klingman, *Walls*, 123.

16. *Tallahassee Floridian*, 2 Apr. 1878.

17. *Tallahassee Floridian*, 7, 28 May, 11, 25 June, 16 July 1878.

18. *Tallahassee Floridian*, 6 Aug., 1 Oct., 12 Nov. 1878.

19. Florida, *Journal of the Tenth Session*, 4, 92-93; Williamson, *Florida Politics*, 46-49.

20. Florida, *Journal of the Tenth Session*, 162.

21. On routine procedural motions, see for example, Florida, *Journal of the Tenth Session*, 37, 43, 56, 66, 74, 99, 124, 152, 164, 447, 449, 475, 634.

22. Florida, *Journal of the Tenth Session*, 76, 131; "Nineteenth Century Florida State Legislature [General Assembly] Resolutions," No. 26, 1879, Box 17, Folder 1.

23. S.B. Conover to Hon. John Sherman, 8 June 1879, John Sherman papers, vol. 175. Conover's estimates of his support within the party were far off the mark.

24. *Tallahassee Floridian*, 6 May 1879; White, *Republican Era*, 11, 110.

25. J.M. Currie, Collector, to John R. Bradford, 26 Mar. 1880; J.M. Currie, Collector, to Hon. Secretary of the Treasury, 16 Mar. 1880; J.M. Currie to J.E. Proctor, 26 Mar 1880; S.D. Mills to James Williamson, 14 Mar., 1882; Collector of Customs at St. Marks, Letters Sent, RG 36, National Archives; Parker, "The Proctors," 28. There is no correspondence from Conover, probably because he was in Washington during the time surrounding Proctor's appointment. See A.A. Knight to S.B. Conover, addressed to Willard's Hotel, 6 Mar. 1880, John Sherman Papers, vol. 210. The collector for the district was headquartered in Cedar Key and the deputy collector's position (head of staff in St. Marks) did not require Senate confirmation.

26. LCDB BR·523; LCTR, 1870, 96. The house survived until the 1970s.

27. For the corrections see J.M. Currie to Proctor, 20 Aug., 20, 25 Sept., 19 Oct., 2 Dec. 1880. The commendatory report is in Currie to Hon. Sec. Of Treasury, 27 Sept. 1880. All citations are to Letters Sent, Collector of Customs at St. Marks.

28. Williamson, *Florida Politics*, 61-63.

29. *Tallahassee Floridian*, 3, 14, 17 Sept., 5 Nov. 1880.

30. Williamson, *Florida Politics*, 66-70; *Tallahassee Floridian*, 2 Nov., 28 Dec. 1880.

31. S.D. Mills, Acting Collector, to John E. Proctor, 14 Mar. 1882, Letters Sent, Collector of Customs at St. Marks.

32. John Wallace and William Stewart were two who were attracted. Williamson, Florida Politics, 83-85.

33. *Jacksonville Daily Florida Union*, 28 May 1882.

34. Williamson, *Florida Politics*, 84-85; *Tallahassee Floridian*, 20 June 1882.

35. It is not known whether or not Proctor was a delegate. As the Democrats became more confident and as Charles Dyke increasingly withdrew from management of the *Floridian*, that paper gave less attention to Republican politics: Republican proceedings were generalized rather than reported in detail. Unfortunately, there are few other newspapers that survive from that time period. The narrative of larger events here is taken from Williamson, *Florida Politics*, 19-95.

36. *Tallahassee Floridian*, 5, 12 Sept. 1882; Skinner, *Reminiscences*, 155-61. Skinner was a conservative businessman and thoroughgoing racist.

37. *Tallahassee Floridian*, 26 Sept., 14 Nov. 1882. George Proctor, John's brother, was elected to the Assembly from Jefferson county.

38. Florida, *Journal of the Twelfth Session*, 43, 239-40.

39. Florida, *Journal of the Twelfth Session*, 74, 93, 142-43, 185, 280, 289, 424.

40. Ibid., 133, 274, 277, 574; *Tallahassee Floridian*, 23 Jan. 1883.

41. Williamson, *Florida Politics*, 96-102, 114; *Tallahassee Floridian*, 22 Apr., 6 May, 29 July 1884. No list of delegates to either meeting survives. Thus, whether Proctor attended is unknown.

42. *Tallahassee Floridian*, 29 July, 16 Sept., 11 Nov. 1884.

43. Florida, *Journal of the Thirteenth Session*, 19, 320.

44. *Tallahassee Floridian*, 20, 23 Apr., 4 June 1885. George Proctor was an unsuccessful candidate for the convention from Jefferson County.

45. *Tallahassee Floridian*, 9, 16, 23 Sept., 14, 21 Oct., 11 Nov. 1886.

10. AFTERWORD

1. Lettie [Proctor] Hill, oral history interview.

2. *Tallahassee Floridian*, 12 Aug. 1884, 26 Mar. 1885, 22 Mar. 1888, 4 Feb. 1890. Construction of hotels, amusement facilities, and restaurants for blacks by blacks was highly significant. On the one hand it gives evidence of the beginnings of a black class of small entrepreneurs and on the other confirms that equal access to public facilities was no longer a significant goal.

3. Ibid., 26 Nov. 1892, 29 May 1902, 24 July, 4 Dec. 1903.

4. Tenth U.S. Census (1880), population schedules for Leon

County, Fla., ED 88, Sheet 37; LCMB 2:289; LCTR, 1890. The population schedules for the Eleventh U.S. Census (1890) are not extant.

5. Lamb, "John Proctor," refers to the bitterness having been transcended.

6. See, for example "LEON COUNTY REPUBLICANS' APPEALS TO THEIR FRIENDS THROUGHOUT THE STATE." Printed one page document, undated but after 1899. Personal correspondence, E.C. Weeks papers. Changing racial attitudes and political conditions in Tallahassee resulted in the virtual disappearance of newspaper interest in black politicians and political interests. Proctor's name was placed in nomination for the legislature in the 1888 Republican convention. No delegate voted for him. The eventual nominees for state and local offices included no black straightouts. *Tallahassee Floridian*, 18 Sept. 1888.

7. "A Brief History of St. Michael and All Angels Episcopal Church," 5; Langhorne's interview of John Proctor.

8. LCMB MM:417, VV:107.

9. Twelfth U.S. Census (1900), population schedules for Leon County, Fla., ED 85, Sheet 8; Leon County Marriage [colored] Book 2:84 and 5:184.

10. LCDB PP:38; LCOR 3:355, 27:112, 29:89, 34:211, 37:187; Leon County Marriage [colored] Book 3:39, 1:222.

11. Twelfth U.S. Census (1900), Population Schedules, Florida, Jefferson County, ED 62, Sheet 13, ED 62 Sheet 5; LCDB 2:235; LCMB 00:103, PP:302, QQ:192, SS:224, 599, UU:238, 501.

Bibliography

PRIMARY SOURCES

Allen, Benjamin F. "A Natural Death," *Florida Sentinel*, 3 July 1855.

Ball, Le Roy D., and John Bradford. Land-ownership Map of Leon County, 1883. Florida State University Library, Tallahassee. Photocopy.

Conover, Simon B. Letter to My dear sir. 24 June 1873. Florida State Archives, Tallahassee.

Escrituras. East Florida Papers. St. Augustine Historical Society. Microfilm.

Finlayson, Edwin H. Letter to Malcomb Johnson. In author's possession. Undated. Copy.

Hill, Lettie [Proctor]. Oral History Interview Transcript. 1975. Junior League of Tallahassee. Florida State Archives, Tallahassee.

Koepen, R.C. Letter to Curtis E. Peterson. 5 Nov. 1973. Historic Tallahassee Preservation Board.

Langhorne, J.L. Interview of John Proctor. In Black Archives, Florida A & M University, Tallahassee.

Parrish Register, 1832-1913. St. John's Episcopal Church. Tallahassee, Fla.

Peterson, Curtis E. Letter to the author. 17 Nov. 1975. Historic Tallahassee Preservation Board.

Pine Hill Plantation Papers. Strozier Library. Florida State University, Tallahassee.

Scott, George Washington. Collection of papers. Florida State Archives, Tallahassee.

Sherman, John. Papers. Library of Congress, Washington, D.C.

Weeks, E.C., and E.H. Weeks. Papers. Florida State Archives, Tallahassee.

Government Documents

"Bureau of Refugees, Freedmen and Abandoned Lands, Records of Sub Assistant Commissioner: Teachers School Reports, Florida." Vol. 21. Record Group 105. National Archives, Washington, D.C.

"Department of Treasury, Collectors of Customs." Record Group 56. National Archives, Washington, D.C.

"Freedmans Savings and Trust Company, Tallahassee Office." Register of Signatures of Depositors at Branches, 1865-1874. Record Group 101. National Archives, Washington, D.C.

Florida. *Journal of the Proceedings of the Assembly . . . at its Sixth Session.* 7 January 1873. Tallahassee: S.B. McLin, State Printer, 1872 [misdated].

———. *Journal of the Proceedings of the Assembly . . . at its Seventh Session.* 6 January 1874. Tallahassee: Harrison Jay, State Printer, 1874.

———. *Journal of the Proceedings of the Assembly . . . at its Eighth Session.* 5 January 1875. Tallahassee: Printed at the Office of the Floridian, 1875.

———. *Journal of the Proceedings of the Assembly . . . at its Tenth Session.* 5 January 1879. Tallahassee: C.D. Dyke, Sr., State Printer, 1879.

———. *Journal of the Proceedings of the Legislative Council at its Eleventh Session.* 7 January 1833.

———. *Journal of the Proceedings of the Senate . . . at the Twelfth Session of the of the Legislature.* 2 January 1883. Tallahassee: Charles E. Dyke, State Printer, 1883.

———. *Journal of the Proceedings of the Senate . . . at the Thirteenth Session of the Legislature.* 6 January 1885. Tallahassee: Charles E. Dyke, State Printer, 1885.

Jefferson County Records. Florida State Archives, Tallahassee.

———. Deed Book Index. 1827-1933.

———. Tax Rolls. 1862-1879.

Leon County Courthouse, Tallahassee, Fla. County Records.

———. Deed Books (LCDB). 1825-1939.

———. Judgment and Execution Docket. 1830-1860.

———. Law Files (LCLF). 1825-1935.

———. Marriage [colored] Book. 1865-1898.

———. Minute Book. Vols. 2-5.

———. Mortgage Books (LCMB). 1825-1961.

———. Official Records (LCOR). 1961-1989.

———. Probate Files. 1840-1898.

———. Tax Rolls. Microfilm. 1860-1878.

"Nineteenth Century Florida State Legislature Documents." Record Group 915. Series 887. Florida State Archives, Tallahassee.

Proctor, Antonio. [Claim] Confirmed by Commissioners. American State Papers. Vol. 4. Descriptive List No. 256, Report 1, No. 21. Bureau of Land Records, Department of Natural Resources, Tallahassee, Fla.

St. Johns County, Fla., Deed Books (SJCDB). Florida State Archives, Tallahassee. Microfilm.

"Talk of Tuskegee Tustumugee to Col. Benjamin Hawkins, (18 September 1812)." *State Papers and Publick Documents of the United States from the Accession of George Washington to the Presidency, Exhibiting a Complete View of Our Foreign Relations Since That Time.* Vol 9. 2nd ed. Boston: T.B. Watt and Sons, 1817.

Tuolumne County Courthouse, Sonora, Calif. County records.

———. Sonora City Burial Record. Vol. 1.

———. Deed Books (TCDB) 1, 10, and A.

———. Inquest #22.

———. Judgment Book C.

———. Judgment Dockets B and C.

———. Tax Rolls. 1852.

———. Transcript of Judgment Book 2.

U.S. Congress. House. *Executive Documents.* 39th Cong., 1st sess.

U.S. Bureau of the Census. Population Schedules of the Fifth (1830) through Twelfth (1900) Census of the United States. Population Schedules for Florida (Jefferson, Leon, and Wakulla counties) and California (Tuolumne). National Archives and Records Service, Washington, D.C.

Territorial Papers of the United States. Ed. Clarence C. Carter and John Porter Bloom. 27 vols. U.S. Department of State. Washington, D.C.: Government Printing Office, 1934-1969.

U.S. Congress. Senate. Committee on Indian Affairs. 30th Cong. 1st sess.

Wakulla County Records. Florida State Archives, Tallahassee.

———. Deed Books. 1842-1892.

———. Tax Rolls. 1863-1880.

SECONDARY MATERIALS

Abbey, Kathryn T. "Lafayette and the Lafayette Land Grants." *Annual* [of Tallahassee Historical Society] (1934): 1-9.

Arnett, Bishop Benjamin W., ed. *Proceedings of the Quarto-Centennial Conference of the African M.E. Church of South Carolina at Charleston, S.C., May 15, 16, and 17, 1889.*

Bartlett, Richard A. *The New Country.* New York: Oxford Univ. Press, 1974.

Berlin, Ira. *Slaves Without Masters: The Free Negro in the Antebellum South.* New York: Pantheon, 1974.

Brady, Dorothy S. "Relative Prices in the Nineteenth Century." *Journal of Economic History* 24:145-203.

Breen, T.H., and Stephen Innes. *"Myne Owne Ground:" Race and Freedom on Virginia's Eastern Shore, 1640-1676.* New York: Oxford Univ. Press, 1980.

"A Brief History of St. Michael and All Angels Episcopal Church." Pamphlet. In *Dedication of Parish Canterbury House and Twelfth Anniversary of the Priest.* In Black Archives, Florida A & M University. Published by the church, 1959.

Buckbee, Edna Bryan. *Saga of Old Tuolumne.* New York: Press of the Pioneers, 1935.

Burton, Orville Vernon. *In My Father's House Are Many Mansions: Family and Community in Edgefield, South Carolina.* Chapel Hill: Univ. North Carolina Press, 1985.

Castlenau, Comte de. "Essay on Middle Florida, 1837-38." Trans. Arthur R. Seymour. *Florida Historical Quarterly* 26: 199-255, 300-324.

"The Charles Hutchinson Letters From Territorial Tallahassee, 1839-1843." Ed. James T. Campbell. *Apalachee* 4:16-17.

Christman, Enos. *One Man's Gold: The Letters and Journals of a Forty-Niner.* New York: Whittelsey, 1930.

Clough, C.S. *A Directory of the City of Tallahassee, Florida.* Tallahassee: T.B. Hilson, State Printer, 1904.

Coker, William. "Entrepreneurs in the British and Spanish Florida." In *Eighteenth-Century Florida and the Caribbean,* ed. Samuel Proctor. Gainesville: Univ. Presses of Florida, 1976.

Cox, Merlin G. "Military Reconstruction in Florida," *The Florida Historical Quarterly* 46:219-33.

Current, Richard N. *Three Carpetbag Governors.* Baton Rouge: Louisiana State Univ. Press, 1967.

Curry, Leonard P. *The Free Black in Urban America, 1800-1850.* Chicago: Univ. of Chicago Press, 1981.

Davis, David Brion. *The Problem of Slavery in Western Culture.* Ithaca: Cornell Univ. Press, 1966.

Davis, William Watson. *The Civil War and Reconstruction in Florida.* New York: Columbia Univ. Press, 1913. Facsimile edition. Gainesville: Univ. Florida Press, 1964.

Dodd, Dorothy. "Bishop Pearce and the Reconstruction of Leon County." *Apalachee* (1946): 5-12.

———. "The Corporation of Tallahassee." *Apalachee* (1948-1950): 80-96.

———. "Old Tallahassee." *Apalachee* (1957-1962): 63-71.

Doherty, Herbert J., Jr. *Richard Keith Call.* Gainesville: Univ. of Florida Press, 1961.

———. *The Whigs of Florida, 1845-1854.* Gainesville: Univ. of Florida Press, 1959.

Donald, David. *Charles Sumner and the Rights of Man.* New York: Knopf, 1970.

Eastland, Mary B., and N. Paul Anthony. *Randall-Lewis House.* Tallahassee: Historic Tallahassee Preservation Board. 1977.

Eppes, Susan Bradford. *The Negro of the Old South: A Bit of Period History.* Chicago: Joseph G. Branch, 1925.

———. *Through Some Eventful Years.* Macon, Ga.: J.W. Burke, 1926.

The Florida Legislature (Twelfth Session) An Unofficial Directory of State Government. Ed. and comp. J.V. Drake. Jacksonville: Times Union Book and Job Office, 1883.

Foner, Eric. *Reconstruction: America's Unfinished Revolution, 1863-1877.* New York: Harper & Row, 1988.

Franklin, John Hope. "James Boon: Free Negro Artisan." *Journal of Negro History* 30:150-80.

Garvin, Russell. "The Free Negro in Florida Before the Civil War." *Florida Historical Quarterly* 46:1-18.

Gatewood, Willard B., Jr., ed. *Slave and Freeman: The Autobiography of George L. Knox.* Lexington: Univ. Press of Kentucky, 1979.

Groene, Bertram. *Antebellum Tallahassee.* Tallahassee: Florida Heritage Foundation, 1971.

Gudde, Erwin G. *California Gold Camps.* Ed. Elisabeth K. Gudde. Berkeley: Univ. of California Press, 1975.

Gutman, Herbert G. *The Black Family in Slavery and Freedom, 1750-1925.* New York: Pantheon, 1976.

Hall, Robert La Bret. "Do Lord, Remember Me: Religion and Cultural

Change Among Blacks in Florida, 1565-1906." Ph.D. diss., Florida State University, 1984.

———. "The Social Cosmos of Black Churches in Tallahassee, Florida, 1865-1885." Master's thesis, Florida State University, 1972.

Harvey, Karen. "Antonio Proctor, A Piece of the Mosaic." *El Escribano* 17:47-58.

Haskins, C.S. *The Argonauts of California: Being the Reminiscences of Scenes and Incidents That Occurred in California in the Early Mining Days by A Pioneer.* New York: Fords, Howard & Harlbert, 1890.

Hoogenboom, Ari. *The Presidency of Rutherford B. Hayes.* Lawrence: Univ. Press of Kansas, 1988.

Jordan, Winthrop D. "American Chiaroscuro: The Status and Definition of Mulattoes in British Colonies." *William and Mary Quarterly* 19:184-89.

Klingman, Peter. *Josiah Walls: Florida's Black Congressman of Reconstruction.* Gainesville: Univ. Presses of Florida, 1976.

Lamb, De Witt. "John Proctor." In Black Archives, Florida A & M University, Tallahassee. Typescript.

Lapp, Rudolph M. *Blacks in Gold Rush California.* New Haven: Yale Univ. Press, 1977.

Litwack, Leon F. *Been in the Storm So Long: The Aftermath of Slavery.* New York: Knopf, 1979.

Long, Charles S., comp. *History of the A.M.E. Church in Florida.* Philadelphia: A.M.E. Book Concern, 1937.

McAlister, Lyle N. *Spain and Portugal in the New World, 1492-1700.* Minneapolis: Univ. of Minnesota Press, 1984.

Meador, John A. "Florida Political Parties, 1865-1877." Ph.D. diss., University of Florida, 1964.

Murat, Achille. *A Moral and Political Sketch of the United States of North America.* London: Effingham Wilson, 1833.

Neyland, Leedel W. "The Free Negro in Florida." *Negro History Bulletin* 29:2-8.

Neyland, Leedel. *The History of Florida Agricultural and Mechanical University.* Tallahassee: Florida A & M University, 1963.

———. *Twelve Black Floridians.* Tallahassee: Florida A & M University Foundation, 1970.

Owen, Leslie Howard. *This Species of Property: Slave Life and Culture in the Old South.* New York: Oxford Univ. Press, 1976.

Paisley, Clifton. *From Cotton to Quail: an Agricultural Chronicle of Leon County.* Gainesville: Univ. of Florida Press, 1967.

———. "How to escape the Yankees: Maj Scott's letter to his Wife at Tallahassee, March 1864." *Florida Historical Quarterly* 50:53-61.

———. *The Red Hills of Florida, 1528-1865.* Tuscaloosa: Univ. of Alabama Press, 1989.

Palmer, Henry E. "The Proctors—A True Story of Ante-Bellum Days and Since," *Annual* [of Tallahassee Historical Society] (1934): 14-16.

Parker, Rosalind. "The Proctors—Antonio, George, and John." *Apalachee* (1946): 19-29.

Patterson, Ruth Polk. *The Seed of Sally Good'n: A Black Family of Arkansas, 1833-1953.* Lexington: Univ. Press of Kentucky, 1985.

Peek, Ralph L. "Curbing Voter Intimidation in Florida, 1871." *Florida Historical Quarterly* 43:333-48.

———. "Election of 1870 and the End of Reconstruction in Florida." *Florida Historical Quarterly* 45:352-68.

Porter, Kenneth W. "Negroes and East Florida Annexation." *Journal of Negro History* 30:18-19.

Proctor, John. Interview. In Black Archives, Florida A & M University, Tallahassee. Photocopy. Typescript.

Proctor, John. Interview. Federal Writers' Project. In P.K. Yonge Collection. University of Florida Library, Gainesville. Typescript.

Richardson, Joe M. "The Freedman's Bureau and Negro Labor in Florida." *Florida Historical Quarterly* 39:167-74.

———. "Jonathan C. Gibbs: Florida's only Negro Cabinet Member." *Florida Historical Quarterly* 42:363-68.

———. *The Negro in the Reconstruction of Florida, 1865-1877.* Tallahassee: Florida State University, 1965.

Roberts, Derrell. "Social Legislation in Reconstruction Florida." *Florida Historical Quarterly* 43:349-60.

Shofner, Jerrell H. "Constitution of 1868." *Florida Historical Quarterly* 41:356-74.

———. "Fraud and Intimidation in the Florida Election of 1876." *Florida Historical Quarterly* 42:321-30.

———. *Nor Is It Over Yet: Florida in the Era of Reconstruction, 1863-1877.* Gainesville: Univ. Presses of Florida, 1974.

———. *History of Jefferson County.* Tallahassee: Sentry, 1976.

Skinner, Emory Fiske. *Reminiscences.* Chicago: Vestal, 1908.

Smith, Julia Floyd. *Slavery and Plantation Growth in Antebellum Florida; 1821-1860.* Gainesville: Univ. of Florida Press, 1973.

Stauffer, Carl. *God Willing: A History of St. John's Episcopal Church, 1829-1979.* Tallahassee: St. John's Episcopal Church, 1984.

Tappan, John S. to "My very dear cousin." Letter. *Florida Historical Quarterly.* 24:108-11.

Tebeau, Carlton. *A History of Florida.* Coral Gables: Univ. of Miami Press, 1971.

Temin, Peter. *The Jacksonian Economy.* New York: Norton, 1969.

Thomas, David Y. "The Free Negro in Florida Before 1865." *South Atlantic Quarterly* 10:335-45.

Thomason, Arthur W. *Jacksonian Democracy on the Florida Frontier.* Gainesville: Univ. of Florida Press, 1961.

Walker, Juliet E.K. *Free Frank: A Black Pioneer on the Antebellum Frontier.* Lexington: Univ. Press of Kentucky, 1983.

Wallace, John. *Carpet-bag Rule in Florida: The Inside Workings of the Reconstruction of Civil Government in Florida After the Civil War.* Jacksonville: Da Costa, 1888. Fascimile edition. Gainesville: Univ. of Florida Press, 1964.

Watson, Thomas Davis. "Merchant Adventurer in the Old Southwest: William Panton, The Spanish Years, 1773-1801." Ph.D. diss., Texas Tech University, 1972.

White, Leonard. *The Jacksonians: A Study in Administrative History, 1829-1861.* New York: Macmillan, 1956.

———. *The Republican Era: A Study in Administrative History, 1869-1901.* New York: Macmillan, 1958.

Williams, Roger M. *The Bonds: An American Family.* New York: Atheneum, 1971.

Williamson, Edward C. *Florida Politics in the Gilded Age, 1873-1893.* Gainesville: Univ. Presses of Florida, 1976.

Wright, Homer Edward. "Diplomacy of Trade on the Southern Frontier: A Case Study of the Influence of William Panton and John Forbes, 1784-1817." Ph.D. diss., University of Georgia, 1972.

NEWSPAPERS

Daily Florida Union. Jacksonville, Fla. 30 June 1876-31 Dec. 1877.

Daily Picayune. New Orleans, La. 7 Feb.-2 June 1849.

Florida Times Union. Jacksonville, Fla. 20 Nov. 1881-30 Dec. 1886.

Gazette & Southern Mines Advertiser. Columbia, Calif. 5 Mar. 1853-25 Apr. 1857.

San Francisco Elevator, San Francisco, Calif. 30 Oct. 1868, 15 Jan. 1869.

Sonora Herald. Sonora, Calif. 3 Feb. 1850-1 Mar. 1856.

Star of Florida. Tallahassee, Fla. 17 Feb. 1838-26 Dec. 1845 (issues missing).

Tallahassee Sentinel (title varies). 4 Nov. 1841-18 Apr. 1843; 4 Nov. 1845-22 Dec. 1855; 14 Jan. 1862-30 Dec. 1876 (issues missing).

Watchman of the Gulf. Apalachicola, Fla. 12 Aug. 1843-28 Oct. 1843.

Weekly Floridian (title varies). Tallahassee, Fla. 1828-1893.

Index

Allen, Benjamin, 61, 87
Allen, Richard C., 35-36
Ames, Willy, 89
Archer, James, 87

Ball, LeRoy, 115-16, 117, 119
Baltzell, Thomas, 31
Bartlett, Washington, 69
Billings, Liberty, 100
Bloxham, William, 99, 127
Bond, Henry, 34
Bryan, Leah, 31

California: black persons in, 68, 71, 75;
    lure of, 68; society in flux, 68, 72
Call, Richard K., 29, 35
Call, Wilkinson, 124
carpetbaggers, 93, 97-98
Cash, W.T., 138
Chaires mansion, 40-42
Chandler, Mary, 47, 52-53, 62
civil rights bill (Florida, 1873), 107
Civil War, in Tallahassee, 88-89
coalition politics in Leon County,
    112-13, 117-18, 121, 134
Colored Convention (1877), 121-22
Congress, U.S., takes control of
    Reconstruction, 92
Conover, Senator Simon: character,
    101-102; constitutional
    convention, 133; customs,
    inspector of, 125; Hayes's policy
    advocate, 121-22; Independency,

opposes, 129; political
    maneuverings, 103-104, 119-20,
    123-27; Sherman, John, supporter
    of, 125; Speaker of Assembly, 105.
    See also, coalition politics in Leon
    County
constitutional revision (Florida), 131,
    133

Demilly, John, 47, 51
Democratic party (Reconstruction),
    105, 116-17, 124, 127, 130
Du Val, Alexander F., 47, 51
Du Val, William P., 22, 24, 26-27, 64
Dyke, Charles E., 98-99, 100-101, 106,
    108, 116, 117

Florida (ship), 71
Florida house, 74-75, 77
Floridian (newspaper), 100
free blacks, 29, 34-35
Freedmen's Bureau, 92

Gibbs, Jonathan, 98, 107
Green Springs Rancho, 72

Hannah, Timothy, 113
Hart, Jason, 66, 88
Hart, Ossian, 103, 177
Hayward, Richard, 55
Hayward, Thomas, 55, 69
Hicks, William, 113

Independency, 128-33

Jay, Hamilton, 108
Jones, Charles W., 114

Lafayette, Marquis de, 27
land values in Tallahassee, 30
Leon County black population, 97
Lewis, B.C., 89, 133
Lewis, Romeo, 36
Lively, Matthew, 89-90, 131

McMullin, George, 69
McQuaig, Daniel, 23
Martin, Malachi, 109-10
Marvin, William, 90
Maxwell, John, 66, 69
Mosely's patent sash lock, 66

Nichols, H.H., 75
Nucleus (Tallahassee), 35-36

Osborn, Thomas, 99

Page, Rev. James, 98, 100
Panic of 1843, 50-51
Panton, Leslie and Company, 16
Pearce, Charles H. (Bishop), 98, 100, 103-104
Proctor, Antonio: death, 79; early life, 16-24; family, 18-20; gains freedom, 18-19; memorial to Congress, 63-67; military service, 18, 19, 22, 29; move to Tallahassee, 24; patrons and friends, 22-23; religion, 49; social status, 18-19, 22, 24, 29, 63-64
Proctor, Bahamia: baptism, 69; birth, 49; family, 94-95; later life, 138; marriage, 94-95; sale of, 87-88
Proctor, Carrol (son of John E.), 126
Proctor, Charlotte (daughter of George), 88, 95
Proctor, Florida (daughter of George), 49
Proctor, George: attempt to take family out of Florida, 53; builder, 30, 33, 39-41, 42-45, 54, 57-58; businessman, 31, 32, 34, 37, 43, 46-47, 51, 58-59, 65-66, 72, 74-76,

83; California, decision and travel, 67-69, 71-73; civil rights advocacy, 81-83; death, 84; early life, 19-24; entrepreneurial man, 44-45, 47, 59-60, 78-81; farm work, 58, 61-62, 64-65; financial situation, 51-52, 54-58, 62, 69, 75-78, 83; legal representation, 56-57; marriage and family, 47-49, 69, 78-79, 85-86, 95; memorial to Congress, 63, 66-67; patrons and friends, 34-37, 41, 67, 74; religion, 49; slaves, use of, 43-45, 62, 80; Sonora, life in, 76-78; status as a free black, 34-35, 37, 45, 53
Proctor, George (son of George), 49, 69, 88, 95, 138
Proctor, George, and Company (Florida), 66
Proctor, Georgianna (daughter of George), 49
Proctor, Henrietta (daughter of John E.), 116
Proctor, John (son of John E.), 116, 137-38
Proctor, John Elias (son of George): Assembly, service in, 104-107, 109-10, 112-14, 119, 124-25; early life, 49, 87, 89-90, 93-94, 98; early political work, 93-94, 96, 98-104; last years, 138-39; Leon County politics, 108-109, 111, 118-19, 121, 123, 129-30, 133-34; life after political career, 135-37; marriage and family, 94, 116, 126, 137; other jobs, 115, 120-21, 123, 126-28; parents, relationship with, 10-11; Senate, service in, 130-34
Proctor, Julia (daughter of John E.), 116, 138
Proctor, Letty (daughter of John E.), 126, 135, 138
Proctor, Mahaimen Stewart. *See* Proctor, Bahamia
Proctor, Malinda (wife of John E.), 137
Proctor, Martha Littleton (wife of John E.), 137
Proctor, Mary (daughter of John E.), 116, 138

Proctor, Mary Magdaline (daughter of George), 49, 69, 88
Proctor, Mary Mason (wife of John E.), 94, 137
Proctor, Nancy: character of, 58; letters from California, 78; marriage to George, 47-48; marriage to Samuel Wells, 88; mortgage on, 48, 62; relationship with son John, 10-11; religion, 49; sold, 79, 87
Proctor, Serapia Edinborough (wife of Antonio), 18
Proctor and Company (California), 72
Proctor and Weeden, 43
Proctor family, 1-2
Propinos, Antonio. *See* Proctor, Antonio

Randall-Lewis house, 40-41
Reconstruction: beginnings of, 90-93; black leadership and, 98; black voters during, 92, 97; business attitudes about, 110; end of, 115, 122; national control of, 92
Reed, Harrison, 93
Republican party: blacks in, 104-105; Florida, 92-93, 102-103, 107-11, 119-20, 127, 129-30, 132; Independency, 128-29, 132; Leon County, 99-103, 105, 108, 111-12, 118-19, 127, 130, 132, 134
Richards, Daniel, 100
Ring, 109
Robinson, Isaac, 42
Rutgers, Henry and Jane, 41, 65-66, 69, 86-88

St. Augustine, 17, 21
St. Marks, 61, 126
St. Michaels and All Angels Episcopal Church, 137
Saunders, William, 100
scalawags, 92-93, 97
Scott, George W., 88
Scott, John R., 105
Simmons, William H., 22-23

slavery, 20-21, 43-45
Smith, Lydia, 85-86, 88, 98
Smith, Rev. James, 94, 98
Sonora, 73-77
source material: *Carpet-bag Rule in Florida*, 8-9; local government records, 3-7; manuscript collections, 8; newspapers, 9-10; oral tradition, 10-13; personal statements, 10, 12-13; state, federal records, 7-8
Stearns, Marcellus, 106, 118-19, 129
Stewart, William G., 94, 104, 118, 121, 127, 129-30
Stokes, Rev. John, 98, 101, 118
Stout, Lydia. *See* Smith, Lydia

Tallahassee: centennial celebration, 138; description of, 26-30, 35, 37, 38-39, 88-89; economic distress in, 39, 51; racial attitudes in, 54, 135-36; society in flux, 29
Thompson, Leslie, 35
three sisters, 33-34

Union Bank, 51

Villalonga, Emanuel, 74

Walker, David, 91, 128, 132-33
Walker, George, 35
Wallace, John: *Carpetbag Rule*, 8; at Colored Convention, 121; early life, 98-99; Greenback party, 123; Independency, 129-30; Proctor, John, relationship with, 8; Republican politician, 100, 104-105, 112, 124, 134
Walls, Josiah, 119, 132
Weeden, William, 31, 43
Weeks, E.C., 101, 111, 119, 123, 132
Wells, Rev. Samuel, 88
Westcott, James, Jr., 36, 56-57
Westcott, James D., Jr., 106
Whigs, 36
Williams, Robert, 87
Work, George, 74
Wyatt, Rev. John, 98, 104